I0815485

MIRO VAN VRECKEM

# THE SOURDOUGH BAKING BOOK

FROM SOURDOUGH STARTER
TO STUNNING
BREADS AND PASTRIES

PHOTOGRAPHY
THIERRY VAN VRECKEM

Lannoo

DSQUARED2

# TABLE OF CONTENTS

# RECIPES

# “ARISEN” FROM PASSION AND LOVE

What drives a young man from the outskirts of Brussels to leave all that's familiar in his life behind him and move to the far north of Norway? Where the wild, untamed landscape is bathed in the gentle glow of the northern lights for six months of the year? To choose a simple life there, a life of silence, close to the earth, close to himself?

And there, to discover his calling: the noble art of baking bread. Not simply bread, by any means, but its most ancient and purest expression: sourdough. A living organism that you must breathe life into, feed, nurture, protect. A child of flour and water that will only grow with patience, attention, and love.

I, too, have found my way to this miracle in the time after my retirement—not out of some romantic attraction, mind you, but out of necessity: The energy crisis gradually deprived my community of its best bakers, until the day came I could no longer get the bread that spoke to my soul: honest, artisan sourdough.

It was only when I tried it myself that I understood how demanding the craft is. You must understand the technique, of course; but then, you must devote yourself to it fully. A whole year long I struggled, tried, failed. Until finally, bread came from my oven that filled me with pride—a loaf that I dared to love.

Now I nurture my sourdough every day. I say hello to it in the morning, I check how it's breathing, I give it some flour, water, a drop of honey. It's like a small, defenseless creature that I must feed. Every ten days, the ritual repeats: knead, wait, proof... four times, a whole day long. And then, the next morning: I bake. Three loaves, three little promises. Always with the same excitement in my heart: what will they become?

And so a love was born from necessity. A passion, arisen as slowly as the dough itself. And then I think of Miro: a young life who made the choice for fire and for total commitment. For the hard road, with the unbounded courage of youth. A life that rises as a sourdough rises: lifted by patience, nourished by passion, and imbued with love. For a life like that, I can have only the utmost respect.

WERNER LOENS
*Chief Inspector of the Michelin Guide*
*for the Benelux, 1987–2024*

ELT

# FASCINATED BY BREAD

I was born in Bever, a small, quiet town just on the edge of the Flemish-speaking part of Belgium. It's rural, green, and I'm sure that's where the seeds of my love of nature today were planted; there aren't many places left in Belgium where you find the beauty and tranquillity you can still find in Bever. I was outside a lot, but I spent most of my time growing up at the Kunsthoeve, a wonderful arts and crafts centre. It was an environment full of creativity, where people made something beautiful with their hands and where, from a very early age, I learned what it really meant to look and feel. That atmosphere has always inspired me, and really made me who I am today. At home, we organised cooking camps and art camps. There was always something to do.

I've been fascinated by bread my whole life. I started baking bread, pizzas and cookies at home as a child, and I never stopped. Always with yeast, because it was always available and always worked. For me, yeast is literally child's play. But for a long time, one thing eluded me: the mysterious workings of sourdough. Too difficult, too mysterious, something to learn later.

Thanks to Jan, Andries, and Karolien for all the knowledge you shared with me. You helped me tremendously getting started, and I can still turn to you whenever I need help. I really appreciate that.

When the time came to go to secondary school, I went to the horticultural school in Melle, and there my interest grew for all things soil, crop growing, and homesteading. By age 14, I was starting to foster the dream of living fully self-sufficiently. Books and TV programmes about the untamed wilderness of the wild north excited me terribly, and I consumed them voraciously. I dreamed of moving to Alaska, though that was, of course, unrealistic and far too far away. But my parents understood that it really was my dream, so one summer they decided we would visit Norway. We chose Røros, a historic town in the remote middle of the country. We got to know the town well, and from the age of 15, I travelled there every holiday to work and learn the language and culture.

In the summer, I worked on a farm in Røros. I helped with the cows, sheep and huskies, and learned what it meant to live with nature. The cottage I lived in was not luxurious; it had no real conveniences, or even running water! But what started as a summer holiday gradually became a plan for the future. The farmers who I worked for could see my enthusiasm and commitment, and they welcomed me back every year. And with their help, when I was 17, I got in touch with the Tana videregående skole, an agricultural school all the way in the far north of Norway, on the border with Russia and Finland.

All I had to do was have a few of my school transcripts translated, and to my surprise and delight, they admitted me to attend my final year of secondary school there. In Tana, the world's northernmost school, a place where reindeer were as common as cows were at home, I found exactly what I was looking for: a life close to nature, education that was both practical and meaningful, and room to grow; not only personally, but to literally grow things!

I was the very first Belgian to study there, something I still look back on with pride. My whole time there, I continued baking: at first still adding yeast, perhaps out of habit, but at some point something started to gnaw at me. More and more, I kept hearing about sourdough, that enigmatic "living" bread, slowly fermented, full of flavor and character. But still, I held back. Sourdough still seemed too difficult, too technical, too sensitive. I had no idea where to start, and I kept putting it off as something to get to at some point in the future.

Until the moment came when I just tried it. It was with Karin, a very good friend, a fellow Belgian who lived in Norway. After a lot of trial and error, fits and starts, and a few failures, we finally started to see life in our starter. The bubbles, the unique odour, the movement... they were fantastic. When we baked our first loaf with our own sourdough starter, there was no going back. I had never experienced anything like that alluring sourness, unique texture, and heavenly aroma. I was hooked; completely under the spell of sourdough. What once seemed too difficult to try became my daily ritual, my craft, my passion.

In 2022, I established my bakery ELT Bakeri in the mountain village of Sollia, on the edge of the Rondane, a national park, and officially started selling bread in Norway. Really, the main reason I did was because I missed the good food of Southern Europe. I regret to say that in Norway, most of the food would disappoint most any of us "from the south." There aren't many bakeries at all, and sourdough bakeries? Forget it.

From the beginning, my mission was clear: only sourdough pastries, made only with pure ingredients, locally milled flour, and the most important ingredient: time. My baked goods quickly found their way into local shops, hotels, and markets, as well as directly to customers who really tasted the difference.

The bakery became a place where everything came together: my roots, my Norwegian future, love for the craft, and the quest for simplicity. Later came the international contacts, including with top Italian bakers through Eataly in Turin and Milan. Nowadays, I often get visits from other bakers looking to get started with sourdough. And I'm happy to share what I know with them. I also regularly give courses to dedicated home bakers and dining establishments to help them get started with sourdough bread.

In 2024, I was voted among the top 10 bakers in Norway; I was also nominated for, and made it to the final round, of the "bakery of the year" competition, but I was ultimately disqualified because I didn't have a diploma in baking studies–at least, not then.

So that year I went straight to Amaury Guichon's prestigious Pastry Academy in Las Vegas, where I further developed my skills. I am very grateful that two great chefs, Michel Ernots and Amaury Guichon, make their knowledge available in this academy, which students with a real passion for baking come to from all over the world to learn and to dedicate themselves to developing the most fantastic products. That experience changed my life, not to mention opened a whole new world of baking. Once back in Norway, I expanded my range with new products and improved the quality of the bakery with what I had learned.

When I look back at the journey, it's not the success in business or the sales that I appreciate most. It's the feeling of having introduced people to new things, and having succeeded at that in a tiny mountain village of just a few hundred inhabitants. And here, they appreciate it too.

# THE HISTORY OF SOURDOUGH

## BREAD OF THE ANCIENTS

Sourdough is more than just another way of making bread. It's an ancient tradition, deeply rooted in human history. More than six thousand years ago, even before the earliest civilisations made their mark on the world, humans had already discovered the miracle of natural fermentation.

The oldest traces of fermented bread, dating back to around 3000 BC, are in Egypt, where archaeologists have found baking ovens and bread moulds in tombs, as well as murals showing scenes of bakers at work.

It's very likely this discovery happened by accident: a mixture of ground grain and water forgotten in the sun, perfect conditions for the wild yeasts in the air to begin fermenting the mixture. The result? A leavened, flavorful bread.

This natural, spontaneous fermentation remained the basis for all bread production well into modern times.

## FROM EGYPT TO THE WORLD

The art of sourdough spread, first via trade along the Nile, and later through contact between peoples around the Mediterranean, across Africa, to Asia, and into Europe.

The Greeks elevated the craft of baking and built public bakeries. The Romans later absorbed this knowledge and spread it further via their roads and legions. In the Roman Empire, bread and wine–both products of natural fermentation, by the way–were soon basic staples.

In medieval times, the "daily bread" was quite literal, and literally the foundation of their diet. For the common people, sourdough breads baked with local grains were the primary source of energy. Every community had its own miller and baker, and sourdough was a living cultural heritage. Starters were passed down from generation to generation, cherished as family treasures.

In monasteries, bread baking was refined into a high art. Monks developed techniques to better control fermentation by experimenting with aspects like temperature and hydration; their insights are still the foundation of how we make sourdough bread today.

## THE REDISCOVERY

The industrial revolution changed everything. By the 19th century, baker's yeast had been developed: first in liquid form, later as cubes of fresh yeast. This controlled yeast made bread baking faster and more

**Traditional bread with kamut — see p. 78**

consistent. Gradually, this form of bread superseded sourdough, with its slower fermentation and complex flavors, and traditional breadmaking began to fade into the background.

In the 20th century, especially after World War II, speed and efficiency became primary considerations, and bread became a mass-market product. The delicate art of sourdough breadmaking almost completely disappeared from modern life.

But in the 1970s a renewed interest in artisan bread arose, fuelled by movements that embraced natural foods and local craftsmanship. Bakers began reaching back to old techniques. They rediscovered the power of long fermentation, the deep flavor of sourdough and the magic of bread that is truly alive.

Today, sourdough symbolises a new framework of values: slow, honest, with respect for grain and craft. In a time of renewed focus on sustainability, biodiversity and local food production, sourdough is taking on new meaning.

Artisan bakers are working with ancient grains like emmer, einkorn and spelt, and using historical methods to ferment them. Old mills are once again producing stone-ground flour, and starter cultures are cherished as living heritage. Initiatives like the Puratos Sourdough Library show that the world today recognises that sourdough is not just one way of making bread; it is culture. Put your hands deep into a soft, fermented dough, and you feel it: the same power that the first bakers felt, six thousand years ago.

A sourdough bread is by no means just another loaf. It's a living story that never ends. Every starter we feed, every dough we knead, puts us in contact with thousands of years of history. Sourdough is eternal.

**The sourdough library was primarily established to preserve the biodiversity of sourdoughs.**

## AMBASSADEURS DU PAIN: A GLOBAL MOVEMENT FOR REAL BREAD

Ambassadeurs du Pain arose in France in 2005 out of a love of craftsmanship and a desire to breathe new life into the traditional baking profession. In a world becoming ever more industrialised and focused on expediency, the founders–including some of the biggest names in French baking, such as Dominique Planchot, Pierre Nury and Amandio Pimenta–wanted to build an international network of professionals standing for quality, respect for the product, and the use of natural processes such as sourdough starters and slow fermentation.

Today, the association has members in over 25 countries across Europe, Asia, the Americas, Africa and the Middle East. From France to Japan, from Brazil to Lebanon, and from Canada to South Korea, there are bakers everywhere who have joined the Ambassadeurs du Pain and are promoting the movement's core values. Each country has its own representatives and organises regional or national selections for the international competitions held by the association.

One of their most prominent initiatives is the biennial international competition Le Mondial du Pain, in which teams of bakers from around the world pit their craftsmanship, taste, technique, and innovation against each other to produce the best bread. It is no ordinary competition; it is a celebration of the craft and an opportunity for both new and veteran bakers to enrich and pass on their knowledge.

The association places a high priority on education, with training, workshops and technical exchanges being a strong focus. They publish technical manuals, teach in baking academies, and are committed to preserving ancient grain varieties and using natural fermentation methods like sourdough. Their goal is twofold: to not only bake high-quality bread, but to help consumers to re-learn what good bread is.

What makes the Ambassadeurs du Pain unique is their holistic vision: they approach bread as culture, as tradition, as both an everyday staple and a modern, forward-looking craft. Sustainability, local raw materials, educating the next generation, and the use of sourdough are key features of the movement. Far from being regressive reactionaries, they are future-builders: bakers who believe that the future of bread lies in its past.

In a world where many bakers are having to adapt to unprecedented speed and volume, Ambassadeurs du Pain choose quality, authenticity and time, in the conviction that the power of bread lies in its simplicity, slowness and connection with people. They are reinventing baking as an act of care and pride, with sourdough as the living heart of their mission.

## SLOW FOOD AND SOURDOUGH

Slow Food is a global movement dedicated to promoting food produced ethically, sustainably and authentically. Specifically, the Slow Food movement began in Italy in 1986 in the wake of Italian activist Carlo Petrini's campaign against the opening of a McDonald's in the historic heart of Rome. It became a response to the rise of a "fast food" culture revolving entirely around speed, efficiency, and food as a mass-made product. But the movement's goals quickly expanded to include the preservation of agricultural biodiversity and the restoration of natural heritage.

Sourdough, with its deep roots in the traditional art of baking, plays an important role in the philosophy of Slow Food. It is an example of how artisanal foods, produced slowly and with natural ingredients, not only promote health at the individual level but also preserve biodiversity and cultural traditions.

Slow Food also engages in bread-related activities worldwide, including conservation projects for unique breads or cereals in danger of disappearing in many countries. These efforts are giving old techniques and forgotten flavors a future. It is a way of keeping food cultures alive, with efforts grounded in reality and a focus on the communities working with them.

To the Slow Food movement, sourdough is the embodiment of traditional and sustainable food. It is an icon of local, artisan production, with bakers preparing their dough by hand and embracing the patience of the fermentation process.

One of Slow Food's most important goals is to strengthen local communities by connecting them to their food production. Sourdough bakeries are often small-scale, local businesses that have a direct relationship with their customers and the communities they serve. These bakeries typically rely on local, organic ingredients, and their products reflect the unique flavors and traditions of their region.

# THE BASIS OF A STARTER

The foundation of any sourdough bread is a sourdough starter. Making a sourdough starter the simple way means simply mixing flour and water and letting it ferment naturally. The process creates a living brew of wild yeasts and lactic acid bacteria in the dough, which combine to both make your bread rise and develop a complex of flavors. Sourdough needs to be nurtured daily. Immediately after feeding with flour and water, the sourdough starts fermenting and extracting nutrients from the flour. This causes the sourdough to grow.

But sourdough is more than just a way to make a bread rise. It's an ecosystem of bacteria and yeasts in a symbiotic relationship. This natural fermentation process makes flavors deeper, but also makes the bread easier to digest, and ultimately gives each loaf a unique character. The science behind sourdough offers both hobby bakers and professional chefs the ability to refine the baking process and consistently achieve exceptional results.

A sourdough can last your whole life if you maintain it properly.

The choice of flour has a major influence on the activity and taste of your sourdough. The most commonly used types are listed below.

**Sourdough, ready to use**

| | |
|---|---|
| **White flour** | Wheat flour with a light colour and mild flavor. |
| **Rye flour** | Rich in nutrients, this flour will make a more acidic starter. |
| **Whole-grain rye** | With a coarser texture, this flour can absorb more water than sifted flour. It will make a darker, coarser starter. |
| **Spelt flour** | Contains less gluten and also absorbs slightly less water. This may make your starter feel more runny. |
| **Kamut** | This grain is trickier for beginners to work with. It contains more sugars, so your starter will peak fast. It has a slight nutty flavor that makes for a good combination with wheat or another cereal. Kamut also absorbs less water than rye or wheat, so your sourdough may feel runnier. |
| **Einkorn** | Very rich in nutrients and an excellent choice for feeding your starter. Einkorn will give your sourdough a deeper flavor. It is low in gluten, so your sourdough will collapse faster after peaking. |
| **Emmer** | Gives rich aromas to the bread and an artisanal end result. The bread will be less airy than with modern wheat varieties. |

## WHAT DO YOU NEED?

**Flour:** when starting out with making sourdough yourself, it's best to start with just rye flour. It contains more nutrients than wheat, so it will give your sourdough a good start in life. Once your starter becomes active and reliable, you can change over to a mix of rye and wheat or other grains. This will have an effect on the colour, texture, flavor and acidity of your breads.

The most commonly used starter is the liquid sourdough starter. This means that you always use equal amounts of flour and water when feeding the starter.

- → **Water:** spring water or filtered water is best.
- → **A glass jar or plastic container:** to keep your starter in and let you keep a close watch on the fermentation process.
- → **A metal or wooden spoon or spatula:** for stirring and mixing.

TIP

To feed your starter, always use 50% rye flour and 50% wheat flour as a base. This will give your starter a light brown colour and enough nutrition from the rye.

**Sourdough after feeding**

## STEP-BY-STEP INSTRUCTIONS

**Day 1: A new life**

- → Combine 25 grams of rye flour with 25 grams of lukewarm water in a glass jar or plastic container.
- → Stir well and let the mixture stand, loosely covered with a lid, for 48 hours at room temperature (about 22–23 °C).

**Day 3: Feeding and observing**

- → You may already start to see some light fermentation.
- → Throw away half the starter from day 1 (or use it; see p. 63), keeping 25 grams. Add another 25 grams of rye flour and 25 grams of lukewarm water and stir well.
- → Let it stand, loosely covered, for 24 hours at room temperature (about 22–23 °C).

The starter that you throw away is called the "discard." You can incorporate it into bread dough. This young discard has built up almost no microflora yet, so many bakers throw it away. However, you can knead it into a yeast dough or make pancakes with it (see *Sweet Sourdough, p. 97*).

You are now using the formula 1.1.1 (see p. 17). You will see this formula come up a lot in the sourdough world. It means that your ratio is equal grams of starter (or sourdough), flour and water (25 grams of starter, 25 grams of flour, 25 grams of water).

You will continue to use this formula for making your own starters, at least at the beginning. The stronger your starter becomes, the more you can adjust the formula. Later you can go to 1.2.2, which means twice as much flour and twice as much water as starter. Some true fanatics even go as high as 1.10.10.

### Days 4–10: Stronger growth

→ Throw away another 50 grams today (or use it, as described, in a yeast dough or pancakes), so you go back to 25 grams of sourdough starter. Add another 25 g of rye flour and 25 g of lukewarm water (returning to 1.1.1) and stir well.
→ Let this starter stand, loosely covered, for 24 hours at room temperature (about 22–23°C).
→ Repeat this step daily until (and including) day 10.
→ Your starter should look better every day. You should notice a slightly sour smell.
→ From day 5, it should be rising nicely and forming air bubbles.

If you don't observe any rising after day 5, the most likely reason is that your starter is too cold. Try using warmer water or moving the starter to a warm place, like on top of your fridge.

Still nothing? Then it might be your flour. Try with a different rye flour and continue feeding. You don't necessarily have to start over from scratch, but keep following the steps as described for days 4–10.

The sourdough will extract all the nutrients and sugars from the flour you are now feeding it daily. This will make it start bubbling and rising. Once it has largely used up all the nutrients in the flour, you will see it sink back down. That's a natural signal that it's time to feed it again.

### Day 11: Ready for use

At this point the sourdough should smell pleasantly sour and have an airy, frothy texture.

Now you can use your starter to make your first sourdough bread! Keep in mind that your starter is still very young, which will mean big air pockets in your bread; this is typical of young starters. There is a lot of wild yeast activity going on, but the lactic acid bacteria are not yet balanced. To get them in balance, keep discarding starter and feeding it daily.

**Active sourdough smells pleasantly tangy and has a light, foamy texture.**

### Tip

For the first few weeks of baking with sourdough, add 1% (of the weight of the flour) baker's yeast to the bread dough. This will give you a balanced rise while still keeping the sourdough flavor.

### Further care

By taking good care of your starter and feeding it regularly, you will build a strong and reliable base for all your sourdough breads.

→ Keep discarding 50 grams daily (or incorporate it into a bread dough; see p. 63) and starting again with 25 grams of sourdough. Then go back to adding another 25 g of rye flour and 25 g of lukewarm water and stirring well. The older your starter becomes, the more you can trust the formula. On average, you can expect to be baking nice, airy sourdough breads after 14 days.

- If you want to build up a lot of starter because you need to make several loaves at a time, just feed without discarding any starter: in other words, if you have 75 grams of starter, add 75 grams of flour and 75 grams of water. This will get you to 225 grams. This is in keeping with the 1.1.1. template (see *Day 3: Feeding and observing,* on building up your starter, on p. 15).
- When making a bread dough, it is always important to reserve some starter and not use it all, otherwise you'll have to start all over again.
- Once you've built up a reliable sourdough starter, you can set aside a jar of it in the freezer so you always have something to fall back on if something goes wrong.

Sourdough is also perfect for drying and rehydrating later. This is very easy to do; simply spread a thin layer of your dough on a piece of baking paper and let it dry out in the open air. You can then grind it in a pestle and mortar and store it in a jar for when you need it.

If your sourdough is at room temperature, you should maintain it by feeding it daily. If you don't bake that often, then after day 14 put your sourdough in the fridge and feed it weekly. But before you bake your next bread, let it come back to room temperature two days ahead of time.

## REMINDER

| | Action | Ingredients | What's happening? |
|---|---|---|---|
| **Day 1** | Combine in a glass jar or plastic container. | 25 g flour + 25 g water | Fermentation |
| **Day 2** | Fermentation | | Fermentation |
| **Day 3** | Discard + feed | Discard 25 g starter<br>Feed with 25 g flour + 25 g water | Light fermentation |
| **Day 4** | Discard + feed | Discard 50 g starter<br>Feed with 25 g flour + 25 g water | Light fermentation |
| **Day 5** | Discard + feed | Discard 50 g starter<br>Feed with 25 g flour + 25 g water | Every day your starter will be fermenting faster. |
| **Days 6 to 14** | Discard + feed | Discard 50 g starter<br>Feed with 25 g flour + 25 g water | If your sourdough is already decently active, you can now start baking bread. Keep feeding for a few more days as long as it's growing. |
| **Day 14 -** | **Further care**<br>If you're storing your sourdough cold, you can feed it once per week. If you're storing your sourdough at room temperature, you can feed it daily. The warmer it is, the faster the fermentation will happen. | Discard 50 g starter<br>Feed with 25 g flour + 25 g water | If you want to keep making more sourdough, you don't always have to discard the old starter. Add 1.1.1, 1.2.2 or more to the old starter to build up a lot of dough for multiple loaves quickly. |

### Extra tips

- → If you soak raisins, olives or dried fruit in water and start your sourdough with the water from this infusion, you will get a sourdough that gets active faster because of the many good bacteria on the fruits.
- → During the summer, or if you live in a particularly warm climate, feed your sourdough twice a day.
- → To stop the fermentation, you can put your sourdough in a cool place.
- → Never wash your sourdough jar with soap; just use hot water. Soap will kill the good bacteria, and you don't want that.
- → Clean the inside of your jar now and then to keep your sourdough from getting all too sour.

## OTHER TYPES OF FERMENTATION

### Stiff sourdough starter

Stiff sourdough starter is a sourdough starter with a lot less water than liquid sourdough starter described above. The *stiff levain* has a hydration of 60–70%. It's known for its great flavor and it makes a bread with a somewhat longer shelf life.

### Poolish

Poolish is a type of fermentation based on equal parts water and flour with just a little yeast added. It is commonly used in baguettes and pizza crusts. You can add 30–70% poolish to your dough.

### Biga

Biga is similar to poolish, but has a lower hydration, approximately 60%, which gives you a firmer texture. It is often used for Italian breads such as ciabatta.

Biga is fermented at a lower temperature than poolish in order to allow deeper flavors to develop.

### Sponge

Sponge is a pre-ferment that is made without salt but with yeast and a hydration of approximately 45%. This distinguishes sponge from poolish, which has a hydration of 100%.

### Fermented dough

Fermented dough, or *pâte fermentée,* is a piece of old bread dough or sweet dough saved to knead into a new dough. It can add an extra flavor boost to your next baking project. You can save fermented dough in the fridge for up to a week, and add up to 20% to your next dough. This is a very standard practice for croissant dough.

## DISCARD

Every time you feed a sourdough starter, you take some away to make room for fresh flour and water. This portion you remove is called the "discard." At the beginning, you may feel like this is a waste, because that dough you are discarding is actually a valuable ingredient in itself.

Discard is made up of fermented flour and water, and it's full of flavor. You can use it in virtually any recipe that doesn't require a long rise, from savoury crackers to light and fluffy waffles–even cookies. Because it is already partially fermented, it adds a deep and more acidic flavor to whatever you make with it.

A sourdough starter is, in essence, simply flour and water, so it is basically a kind of general-purpose dough that you can easily incorporate into almost anything, because it will do very little to the consistency of your dough or batter. Pancakes, waffles, crackers, muffins, even cookies–because it is already partially fermented, it will bestow a deeper flavor and more acidic edge to whatever you are making.

It's typical to always keep some discard in the fridge. But be warned, after a few days when all the nutrients are used up it will start to become too acidic. If you want to keep it for longer, you should freeze it.

**Tip**
A handy rule of thumb is: take the weight of your sourdough discard and divide it by two. You can then replace that amount of flour and liquid with your discard in any recipe.

**Using starter in your dough**
When it comes time to knead your dough, start on the first day by putting a portion of your starter in a new jar or container and feeding it with flour and water. This will start fermenting immediately and rise to its peak. This peak is the stage in which the sourdough starter is the most active. The volume has increased and the surface is covered in air bubbles. The odour is funky and lightly acidic. It will reach its highest point just before it falls. That's the moment that your sourdough is ready and you can start kneading.

**Why that exact moment?**
At its peak, the starter is in optimal condition. The yeasts have multiplied and are busily producing carbon dioxide. The lactic acid bacteria have produced acids that are going to give the dough flavor and shelf life. There is a balance between energy and acid, between strength and character. If you add your sourdough to another dough at this moment, then it will act as a powerful catalyst: it activates the dough.

**Why not later?**
If you use the sourdough too late, if it's hungry and starts to fall, then it really won't have the same strength. There's a window of a few hours where you can still use a fallen sourdough, but the yeasts will be less active. If you wait until it has completely fallen, then the acids will dominate–that will mean a slow rise, and a harsh-tasting bread and heavy crumb.

Although you can make a very aromatic bread with this "old sourdough," that requires experience and careful timing. For most breads, certainly if you want the dough to rise nicely and not be too acidic, then you should use the sourdough when it peaks.

You can play with the ratio of the sourdough if you would like to start with the dough later.

| Figure | definition |
|---|---|
| 1.2.2 | 10 g starter, 20 g flour, 20 g water |
| 1.5.5 | 10 g starter, 50 g flour, 50 g water |
| 1.10.10 | 10 g starter, 100 g flour, 100 g water |

This is a good trick if you don't have time right then and need to wait a little longer. Because you're adding more food, it will take longer before your sourdough begins to rise.

## ASSESSING FLOUR

Every type of flour is different, and every producer of flour uses its own ingredients, formulas and mixtures. You can test the quality of flour yourself, and it's good to do this because the less moisture there is in the flour, the more water you can add to your bread.

Simply take a handful of flour and squeeze it into a ball.

→ 12% moisture content = good quality; the ball doesn't hold together.
→ 14% moisture content = medium quality; some of the flour falls out of the ball but some sticks.
→ 16% moisture content = poor quality; the flour stays in a ball.

# AUTOLYSIS

Among the many techniques that bakers have developed down through the centuries, autolysis occupies a special place.

Autolysis is a commonly used technique in the preparation of bread, but it is not always necessary. It is used mainly for breads with a high hydration and for baguette-type loaves.

Autolysis might sound technical, but it's exceedingly simple. To perform an autolysis, you only need two ingredients: all the flour and all the water from your recipe. Mix these together until all the flour is incorporated; simply working it with your hands or a spatula should be sufficient. And then, all you have to do is: nothing. Just let it rest. The gluten will start to form right away, which will make for a more elastic and stronger dough. The autolysis is the rest period after mixing, usually 30–60 minutes, after which you add the salt and sourdough starter.

Letting time do its thing has a number of positive effects that help the baking process along and improve the end result. One of them is the spontaneous natural formation of gluten. This automatically gives you a more elastic dough, which will save you time when it comes to kneading and makes your dough generally easier to handle. Another advantage of autolysis is that it gives your flour the opportunity to fully hydrate; you will be able to add more water, which will lead to a airier crumb.

It also means some advantages on the practical side, for example: in large bakeries, reduced kneading time means energy savings and less wear and tear on the equipment. And dough that is less sticky and easier to handle is easier to shape.

Some people find that after an autolysis, bread has a richer flavor, but this is fairly subjective so your mileage may vary.

**Rising dough, almost ready to use**

**The autolysis technique was introduced in the 1970s by a French baker named Raymond Calvel. He was an expert breadmaker and played a huge role in the improvement of the quality of traditional French bread. Having observed that excessive kneading could damage a dough, leading to diminished flavor and a denser bread, he discovered that leaving a dough to rest after combining the flour and water improved the gluten structure naturally, which also meant that the dough didn't need such intensive kneading.**

# BAKER'S YEAST VERSUS SOURDOUGH

Yeast and sourdough are the twin foundations on which both modern and traditional bread baking are built. But while baker's yeast is an industrial product that has only been widely used since the 19th century, sourdough has existed for thousands of years. In this chapter we look at the differences, the practical effects on the baking process, and the advantages and disadvantages of both systems.

Baker's yeast (*Saccharomyces*) is a single-celled mould that multiplies quickly and gives a powerful rise. In fact, it's the strongest yeast with the strongest rising force you'll find on earth. It's selected and trained like an athlete to produce the best performance during its one mission: making bread.

Sourdoughs, on the other hand, are made up of a complex community of wild yeasts and lactic acid bacteria. Typical yeasts include *Candida milleri* and *Saccharomyces exiguus*, while the bacteria commonly belong to the genus *Lactobacillus*. The interaction between these organisms leads to the production of lactic acid and acetic acid, which give sourdough bread its characteristic scent and flavor, as well as its longer shelf life.

A look at sourdough under a microscope reveals a tremendous variety of cells in all shapes and sizes, often with amino acid bacteria that arrange themselves in chains and yeasts of every shape imaginable. This variation is essential for the complex fermentation profile.

## BAKER'S YEAST VERSUS SOURDOUGH

| Characteristic | Baker's yeast | Sourdough |
|---|---|---|
| **Rise speed** | Very fast | Slower |
| **Flavor depth** | Shallow | Complex, acidic, aromatic |
| **Microbiome** | Monoculture | Polyculture (yeasts + bacteria) |
| **Shelf life of bread** | Shorter shelf life | Ripens slower, lasts longer |
| **Health** | Harder to digest for some people | Potentially prebiotic and easier to digest |
| **Gluten intolerance issues** | More | In some cases, fewer issues (not Coeliac disease) |
| **Control of technical aspects** | High | More difficult to control |
| **Consistency of product** | High consistency | More variable |

## THE CONS

Baker's yeast is built for speed, but that speed leaves less time for the natural breakdown of compounds like phytic acid, which can impede the absorption of minerals. It's also what gives some people who are sensitive to it that "bloated" feeling after eating bread.

Baker's yeast produces primarily carbon dioxide gas, and little to no organic or aromatic acids. That means it gives the bread volume, but because there's so little time between the kneading process and the dough going into the oven, the bread has very little time to develop any flavor.

Bread made with baker's yeast gets hard faster, moulds quicker and has fewer defences against microbial breakdown. And because the yeast is so powerful, the rising time is actually so short that there is not enough time for the process of enzymatic breakdown to actually get going. As a result, phytic acid, which bonds with minerals, is not sufficiently broken down, and this can be a problem for people with sensitive digestion or gut flora issues.

There are also some objections to baker's yeast on a cultural level. It is a standardised monoculture, developed for predictability. In the transition to industrial bakeries, this was of course a logical choice, but one that has in many ways been detrimental to the craft of baking. Breads that derive specific flavors from local yeasts and lactic acid bacteria that defined the character of bread from the region for centuries have been pushed out to make room for the "yeast bread" that, more or less, tastes the same everywhere. A carefully tended and crafted sourdough bread, on the other hand, reflects local traditions and a slower way of life.

Sourdough requires more time, attention and experience. It is more sensitive to temperature fluctuations and requires care and feeding throughout the process. Because it is much less predictable, it is less suited for industrial applications.

## THE PROS

Baker's yeast is fast, cheap and efficient. It gives bakers control over the process and predictable results. For good or ill, it is essentially an absolute must-have for mass production.

Beyond this, yeast is extremely easy to use. Just a small amount is enough to make a dough rise dramatically. The rising process can be precisely timed, making use of the yeast as simple as following the instructions. For beginners, baker's yeast is an ideal introduction to baking with leavened doughs. It opens the door to the world of baking without confronting the complexity of a living sourdough culture.

Additionally, baker's yeast's mild, neutral flavor profile leaves room for other flavor components: in recipes where other ingredients need to dominate, such as

**Cinnamon rolls can be made with either sourdough or yeast.**

brioche, cinnamon rolls and raisin bread, yeast bread's lack of flavors of its own makes it very suitable. The gentle fermentation of yeast respects the sweetness of milk, butter and sugar. In rich doughs like these, baker's yeast has just the right amount of rising force without adding acidity or off-flavors.

Sourdough offers a richer taste experience and a fuller nutritional profile, lasts longer than yeast bread and is a fixture of artisanal and local baking culture. Because of its long fermentation, the gluten in sourdough bread is partially broken down, which makes it easier on the digestive system.

Sourdough's strength lies in its complexity. While baker's yeast goes straight for the goal, sourdough develops a flavor landscape that slowly unfolds in the dough. Lactic acid, acetic acid, alcohols, esters... these are the natural connections that arise during the long fermentation and come together to make a bread with character.

This fermentation also has technical advantages. The biological activity of the sourdough reduces the pH of the dough, which makes the bread last longer and inhibits mould growth. It also helps break down phytic acid, which improves mineral absorption. And during the long fermentation process, gluten structures are partially broken down, which makes sourdough bread easier to digest.

There is also an aesthetic beauty to working with sourdough. Every dough feels different, smells different, reacts differently. It demands attention, experience and time. But it is through this necessarily slow and unhurried process that a connection with the bread and with the craft emerges. Sourdough teaches you to look, smell and feel. It is not purely functional, like yeast, but a living ingredient, and you feel that in every aspect of the bread.

The artisanal baking trend and the growing awareness of issues in nutrition have revitalised interest in and appreciation of sourdough bread. At the same time, baker's yeast remains indispensable in modern bakeries. The future may lie in hybrid systems combining both techniques for optimum flavor and efficiency. We should not see baker's yeast and sourdough as polar opposites; rather, they represent different approaches, each with its own strengths. The modern baker can choose between them or combine them. Some recipes use both: a little yeast to be on the safe side, with a little sourdough for more flavor. Others use exclusively one or the other–sourdough, perhaps to highlight the tradition or for considerations of digestibility, or yeast, for reasons of speed or to obtain that light, airy structure.

The choice, then, is not one between right or wrong, between quick or slow. It is a question of what you're most comfortable with. What do you want to say with your bread? How much time do you want to give the dough? What does the recipe call for, what does the moment call for, what does the customer want? Both approaches have their place–in the bakery, in the book and in the bread.

# KNEADING DOUGH

Kneading is an essential element of the breadmaking process. It creates the structure of the dough and activates the development of gluten, which is critical for retaining gases as the bread rises. Gluten is a protein (or actually several proteins, primarily gliadin and glutenin) that, under the influence of water and mechanical action, forms a network that gives bread its structure. You can tell a well-kneaded dough by its firm, elastic structure; when baked, it produces a smooth, even crumb. This chapter examines the basic principles of kneading, the differences between kneading methods and machines, and how as a baker you learn to assess when a dough is fully developed.

**In a professional context, the dough is kneaded by machine.**

## KNEADING: MAN(UAL) VERSUS MACHINE

**Kneading by hand**

Kneading by hand demands experience, patience and yes, some good old-fashioned muscle power as well. But it's also the best way for both beginning and artisan bakers to get a good feel for how a dough is developing. There are a number of different techniques (the classic "slap and fold", pounding out and then folding back the dough on a work surface, as well as many others), but they all share the same principle: stretch the dough out and then compress it back together to gradually develop the gluten.

Kneading by hand gives you better control of the dough: you feel the resistance, see how the dough is changing, and notice when it's ready to rest. But it's less efficient for larger quantities and much more physically demanding for doughs with higher hydration.

**Kneading by machine**

Most professional environments use some form of machine kneading. It's important to understand here that the various kneading machines work in different ways and deliver different results.

The most common kneading machines:

→ **Spiral kneader:** very common in artisan bakeries. Basically, a turning spiral-shaped arm turns within a rotating mixing bowl. Relatively fast and powerful. A spiral kneader will warm the dough somewhat. They are also available in smaller models for home bakers.

- → **Home kneaders (KitchenAid and others):** There are a great many different types of small kneading machines for home use on the market. If you're choosing one, always go for quality. KitchenAid has a model for everyone, from the home baker to the professional chef. The more powerful KitchenAid models do cost more, but they can handle more dough and knead more efficiently.
- → **Double-arm kneader:** these kneaders are designed to simulate manual kneading. The kneading is slow, but very dough-friendly. They are a better choice for delicate doughs and long fermentations. They also transfer very little heat to the dough. Their main disadvantage is that they need 30–45 minutes for a good kneading.
- → **Planetary mixer:** mixes in a rotary motion around its own axis. It is commonly used in smaller bakeries or confectioners. Less suitable for heavy kneading. A lower-cost solution, but less useful for mixing doughs. Most often used for pastry-making.
- → **Fork kneaders:** not often seen today, and the ones you find are usually older machines. These are very slow, but interesting for extensive fermentations, and they produce supple and stretchable doughs.
- → **Industrial high-speed kneaders:** efficient, but the fast kneading speed transfers heat very quickly into the dough. Some aromas can be lost in this type of machine.

As this should make clear, the speed, intensity, direction of rotation and time required will vary from machine to machine. If you follow a recipe with set kneading times without adjusting for the machine you are using, you may be risking over-kneading or under-kneading. Every baker must get to know their own kneading machine and also learn to recognise when the gluten is fully developed.

## DOUGH TEMPERATURE

During kneading, the friction of the kneading process will cause the temperature of the dough to rise. Too warm, and the rate of fermentation will increase, meaning less control of the ripening and a risk of oxidation of flavor compounds. The ideal temperature for sourdough is around 23 °C. At higher temperatures (in excess of 26–27 °C), you run the risk of over-fermentation and loss of aromas.

### Tips

If your kneader is taking a long time to develop the dough sufficiently, use colder water to avoid overheating. With intensive kneaders that raise the dough temperature quickly, you may need to use water at 5–10 °C to stay within the desired temperature zone.

The ambient temperature is also an important factor to consider. In summer, you should probably always be using colder water, while in the winter it's a good idea to use somewhat warmer water to keep things moving. In tropical countries, bakers are known to use ice cubes instead of water in order to keep the temperature under control.

## LEARNING WHAT TO FEEL AND SEE

Although this book gives instructions about kneading time, for example "3 minutes slow and 6 minutes fast," these are only guidelines. Because of differences in flour quality, hydration, ambient temperature and type of kneader, it is impossible to provide a single, standard kneading time that will work in all circumstances.

You can recognise a well-kneaded dough by:

→ a smooth and homogenous surface,
→ good elasticity, without tearing upon being stretched,
→ a strong, well-developed gluten structure,
→ easily stretchable dough,
→ medium or full gluten development.

One useful tool for checking gluten formation can be the "windowpane test": take a small piece of dough and carefully stretch it out as far as you can. If it forms a thin, nearly transparent film without tearing quickly, you have a good network of gluten. For certain uses, sometimes you can stop kneading when you have a partially well-developed gluten network. The gluten will continue to develop on its own during the first proof (rise).

## OVER-KNEADING AND UNDER-KNEADING

An under-kneaded dough is flaccid, breaks quickly, and does not hold a shape. It is also extremely sticky. An over-kneaded dough, on the other hand, is too stiff, loses its springiness, and is also difficult to shape because it's too hard. When over-kneaded, particularly in fast industrial mixers, the gluten network becomes too well-developed, which then leads to a dense crumb and not enough oven spring, the final burst of activity when the dough goes into the hot oven.

## SUMMARY: TIPS FOR CORRECT KNEADING

→ Determine the desired end temperature of your dough before you start (which will be ± 23 °C).
→ Adjust the temperature of the water based on the environment, the flour type and the kneading machine.
→ Observe the dough and develop a feeling for texture and strength.
→ Know the type of kneader you are using, and adjust kneading time and speed accordingly.
→ Use the times given in this book as a guideline, not as a strict rule.
→ Avoid overheating the dough. If necessary, measure the temperature as you go. If it feels too warm, you can start the first rise in the fridge or freezer to allow the dough to cool off a little.

Kneading is a technique that you must master through experience. Machines can make the job easier, but as a baker you have to learn to see, feel, and understand when the dough is ready for the next step. To teach yourself these things, start by kneading your doughs by hand.

# GLUTEN

Gluten is a network of proteins in wheatmeal that gives the dough structure, elasticity and the ability to hold gas during the rising process. In this chapter we discuss how gluten develops and what techniques the baker can use to create an optimal gluten network.

In most cookbooks and in most cooking classes, kneading is the first commandment. You have to create gluten by kneading intensively: no muscles, no bread. Today, there is growing pushback against that idea. As interest in gluten grows and more research is being done into gluten development, we are learning that time is also a critical ingredient in gluten development. This is what we refer to as autolysis.

Kneading will produce gluten faster, but it will also heat up the dough. And this temperature can be critical; remember that in hotter climates they sometimes add ice to the dough instead of water to keep the dough at the desired temperature.

## GETTING EXTRA TENSION INTO THE DOUGH

**Coil fold**

The coil fold is a gentle kneading technique that is particularly well-suited for doughs with high hydration or made from grains with a fragile gluten network, such

**Low gluten development:** a weak, unelastic dough that breaks down into tiny particles.

**Medium gluten development:** the dough begins to feel firmer, but still medium-grainy.

**Full gluten development:** the dough is fully developed and you can stretch it into a film without it tearing.

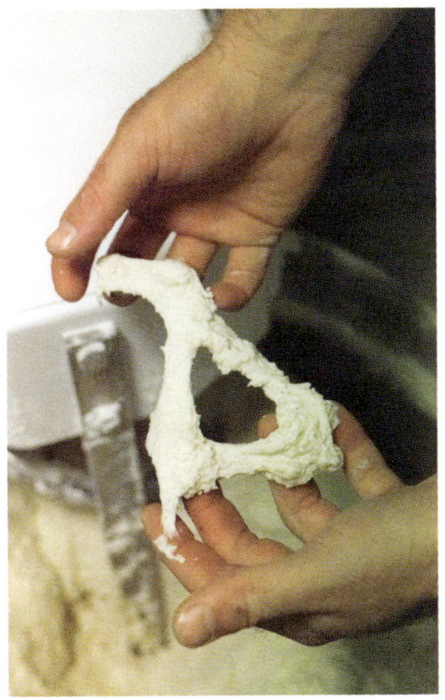

as emmer or spelt. Instead of forcefully stretching and folding the dough, as with the classic "stretch and fold" technique, the coil fold accomplishes the task much more gently. You lift the dough and let it stretch itself under its own weight for each fold. This technique is handiest if you are making multiple loaves, but it is my absolute favorite that I use in every recipe!

Bakers who work with delicate or elastic doughs love the coil fold. It creates tension without forcing the network, and respects the natural structure of the dough. Coil folds strengthen the dough evenly without overtaxing it. The result: a bread with a lovely open crumb.

Performing a coil fold demands attention and a gentle touch. Here's how to do it: First, place your dough in a bowl. With wet or lightly greased hands, carefully lift the dough by the middle. Each side should hang down like loose arms. Gently set the dough back down into the bowl. Now turn the bowl a quarter-turn and repeat.

During the first proof, also known as the "bulk fermentation," you can do this fold a few times, in many cases three, but always allow a break of approximately 30 minutes between each. After each coil fold, the dough will feel noticeably smoother and more even. For some types of dough, just one coil fold will be sufficient, while others will need three or four. This will depend on the flour, the temperature, the moisture content, and your baker's touch.

**By folding the dough in successive layers, you gradually build a strong gluten network without the need for intensive kneading.**

It's a technique that you learn with practice. In the beginning, you'll find that your dough still sticks to your hands, but when you get the feel for the right amount of moisture on your hands you'll notice the difference. This is the craft in its purest form: a dialogue between hand and dough, without words, just complete attention.

### Stretch and fold

The stretch and fold is a classic technique in sourdough baking, and for many bakers is a first step towards working with long-ripened, naturally fermented doughs. It's an action that is simple enough, but has tremendous influence on the ultimate structure, tension and airiness of the bread. By folding the dough into successive layers you gradually build up a strong gluten network without intensive kneading.

In stretch and fold, you first carefully lift up the dough on one side, stretch it out, and then fold it over upon itself. Then rotate the dough a quarter-turn and repeat this movement, then turn again and repeat until you have turned the dough all the way around. You often do this three times every half hour, so: just after kneading, then 30 minutes later, and then again 30 minutes after the second time. Each time the dough has relaxed a bit, you fold again.

What makes this technique so special is how you slowly give strength to the dough. The difference between the first and the last stretch and fold is striking: where the dough was first flaccid, sticky or loose, after a few rounds you will feel significantly more tension and suppleness. This structure is decisive for the volume, the tension and the crumb of your ultimate bread.

Stretch and fold works particularly well at average hydration or with doughs based on wheat or rye that require a certain firmness. With wetter doughs, the technique discussed above (the coil fold) is more suitable: that technique uses less strong folds, but distributes the tension more evenly and more gently. Many bakers use both techniques depending on the character of the dough, with stretch and fold for a robust structure and coil fold for the refined finishing. Every baker has their own favorite technique.

What they all have in common is the rhythm. Between each fold there is a moment of zen in which the dough rediscovers itself: enzymes do their work, bacteria build flavor, and the gluten relaxes momentarily, only to come back stronger. It is this alternation between digging in and letting go that gives the sourdough its many layers of complexity.

### Lamination

Whereas with the classic stretch and fold technique the baker works the dough from the outside in, lamination invites the baker to roll out or stretch out the dough into a thin sheet, approximately one centimetre thick and just strong enough not to tear.

The technique is simple, but demands a certain sensitivity in its execution. After a brief rest, the dough is carefully removed from the mixing bowl and placed on a lightly oiled or floured work surface. With gentle, even movements you then stretch the dough from the centre to the edges, working outwards, to form a rectangle. This surface can then be used to build up tension by folding the dough back on itself in three or four layers, like a letter in an envelope. This creates a "stacked" structure with layers that expand during the baking process, boosting the springiness of the crumb and the volume of the bread.

Lamination is very well-suited for doughs with high hydration, such as ciabatta or focaccia. These are the doughs that are generally difficult to handle at the beginning of the process: they are almost liquid, they are sticky, and they cannot hold a shape.

Lamination also offers great advantages to bakers who add seeds, nuts, herbs or other additions to their dough. By distributing these additions evenly over the rolled-out dough before folding, they will be evenly distributed without overburdening the dough.

What distinguishes lamination from techniques like the coil fold is the direct contact with the dough surface. You see the structure, and you feel in your fingertips how far you can go. You can better read the dough and better feel what it needs.

### Bassinage

*Bassinage* is a French term that, literally translated, means "sprinkling." It is a baker's technique that is often used for doughs with high water content; in short, it means adding a portion of the water only after the dough is already partially developed. Instead of adding all of the water immediately after the first kneading, you reserve 5–15% of the water, which you only add later, once the gluten network has started forming. Using this technique, you can develop very elastic doughs.

With sourdoughs that have a high hydration (80% and above), you will notice very quickly that you are working with very sticky and difficult-to-handle dough. It's hard to shape, it runs, and it's very sticky on your hands.

But once you get working with them, you will get a dough that is more supple, easier to handle, and able to absorb more water without losing its structure.

# BULK FERMENTATION

Bulk fermentation, also referred to as the "first proof," is the phase of fermentation that follows the kneading of the dough. During this phase the dough is developing, gases are being formed, the gluten network is taking shape, and flavors are beginning to appear. For sourdough bread, the bulk fermentation is a critical step that determines the ultimate volume, crumb structure and flavor of the bread.

The bulk fermentation serves multiple functions:

- → **fermentation:** the wild yeasts are producing carbon dioxide gas ($CO_2$), causing the dough to expand.
- → **flavor development:** lactic acid bacteria are converting sugars into lactic acid, acetic acid and aromatic compounds.
- → **gluten development:** the gluten network is relaxing and restructuring itself.
- → **even distribution of ingredients:** a homogenous rise of the dough will mean a consistent structure of the bread.

This phase goes more slowly with sourdough than with bread based on baker's yeast due to the lower concentration of yeasts and the presence of acids.

## FACTORS THAT INFLUENCE THE TIME

The duration of the bulk fermentation depends on a number of different elements.

### Dough temperature after kneading

Higher temperature accelerates the fermentation. You should generally be aiming for a temperature of 23–24°C after kneading. Higher temperatures (> 25°C) lead to faster, but less stable fermentation; lower temperatures (< 22°C) delay the process considerably.

### Ambient temperature

A warm place (25–27°C) shortens the rise. In a cold environment (<20°C) the bulk fermentation can take over five hours.

### Activity and dosage of the sourdough starter

A more active sourdough and/or a higher dosage will result in a faster rise. A young, fresh sourdough will mean a shorter bulk fermentation than an older, acidic one. If you use more sourdough in your breads, you will get a less acidic bread than if you use very little. By using more sourdough, your dough will rise faster, and so have less time to develop flavors.

### Composition of the dough

Fats, sugars and eggs delay the fermentation. Doughs with a high concentration of wholemeal flour will generally ferment faster than white doughs because they have more enzymatic activity.

### Hydration

The higher the hydration, the faster the action of the enzymes, but the more the dough will be sensitive to over-fermentation.

**Guideline:** at a dough temperature of 23–24°C and an active sourdough, the bulk fermentation will generally take between four and five hours at room temperature (20–23°C).

### Characteristics of a properly fermented dough

- → The volume has increased by 35–60%
- → The dough feels airy, supple and slightly elastic
- → Bubbles are visible on the surface
- → You can carefully remove the dough from the bowl without tearing it
- → When you press into the dough, it springs back gently and is not limp

Over-fermentation will give you a sticky, unstable dough that is difficult to shape, and it won't maintain its structure during baking.

Because fermentation is strongly temperature-dependent, both the dough temperature and the ambient temperature must be monitored closely. Use a thermometer to check the dough temperature after kneading. If the dough temperature is warmer than desired, this can be corrected next time by using colder water during kneading.

When the ambient temperature is very warm (in summer, or in very hot climates), it may be necessary to proof the dough in a cooler place or to shorten the bulk fermentation. In summer, the bulk fermentation may be as little as three hours. In cold conditions (winter, or very cold climates) you should leave the dough in a heated space or in a proofing chamber.

**Special attention to sweet and fat-based doughs**

Bulk fermentation of doughs based on fats (butter, oil), sugar or eggs will be slower than with standard bread dough. This is because:

→ sugar binds to moisture and slows down enzyme action.
→ fat relaxes the gluten structure.
→ eggs make the dough heavier and delay fermentation.

**Guideline:** for these doughs, extend the bulk fermentation by at least 30–50% or increase the dough temperature to 25–26°C to compensate for this. In many cases, a warm place for fermentation will be needed to maintain sufficient activity. With sweet sourdough breads, a little yeast is sometimes added to accelerate the rise.

## PRACTICAL TIPS

→ Cover the dough with transparent clingfilm to keep it from drying out while allowing you to still monitor the volume and the gas formation.
→ Work in a space with a stable temperature (20–24°C).
→ Use a digital dough thermometer for precise measurements.
→ To help visually monitor the rise, put a small piece of dough in a glass jar next to your main dough.
→ Try to gain experience by combining visual observation, scent and feel.

The bulk fermentation is an essential phase in the process of making sourdough bread; in this phase the dough is physically, chemically and microbiologically changing. For a successful proof, you must pay attention to temperature, timing and dough assessment. Standard times are only indicative; the baker must decide on the basis of observation when the dough is sufficiently fermented.

A correctly performed bulk fermentation will lead to a well-developed gluten network, a balanced flavor and a dough that is ready to be shaped and have tension built up for the second proof in the fridge.

# SHAPING SOURDOUGH BREADS

After kneading, autolysis, folding, and the first bulk fermentation, it's time for one of the most difficult steps in the sourdough process: shaping. Here you can go in countless different directions. The main reason that we shape the dough is to put tension in the dough, which is crucial to prevent your bread from collapsing during baking.

This step is laying the foundation for the structure, the crust, the oven spring (rise) and, ultimately, the glorious look of your bread.

For many bakers, shaping begins with "pre-shaping," by which the dough is quickly and loosely shaped into a rough round. After a brief rest of 10–20 minutes under a kitchen towel or clingfilm, the baker can assess how the dough is behaving: flaccid, firm, wet or elastic. After this rest period you can give your bread its ultimate shape.

Batard, baguette or boule? Whatever the shape, the goal is always the same: to preserve tension on the outside, stability on the bottom and airiness on the inside. How to do all this? Very carefully! It's extremely important to handle the dough gently at this stage, since the last thing you want to do is to push out all those nice bubbles in the dough that you and your starter have spent hours making.

To make a round loaf (boule), first stretch the dough out and under itself, turning with your hands or using a dough scraper. Here every movement is focused on creating a smooth surface without forcing the dough. For an oval loaf (batard), you first spread the dough out into a rectangle, then fold the sides in, and then finally roll the dough up with your hands and seal and tension it with your palms.

What is absolutely crucial is keeping as much air in the dough as possible, especially in the case of a well-fermented sourdough. Any excessive pressure will lose the bubbles and result in a too dense crumb. Having said that, your dough can't be too relaxed either, because then it will fall during baking and you'll get a very thick pancake.

Shaping a dough with high hydration requires a different approach than a firmer dough. Wet doughs can feel sticky and runny, so shaping them is a more subtle and rhythmic affair, which you will need to do with wet hands. Sometimes you will need to build up tension with multiple short, folding movements, allowing rest time between each. Here you will be glad if you used the coil fold technique at the bulk fermentation stage, because you will have reinforced your structure in advance.

Doughs based on whole grain flour, emmer, or any variety of heritage grain also require extra attention: these will generally be more fragile, break more quickly if tension is too high, and respond better to shorter and more gentle (but effective) shaping movements.

After shaping, most bakers will lightly dust their dough with flour and set it aside in a proofing basket, with the seam facing up. This way, all you have to do is turn out the proofing basket and your dough is facing the right way up, ready for the next step.

Step 1: Place the risen dough on a floured work surface.

Step 2: Gently stretch the dough slightly.

Step 3: Fold one side toward the center.

Step 4: Fold the other side toward the center.

Step 5: Fold the top edge forward over the dough.

Step 6: Rotate the dough 90° and fold the sides toward the center.

Step 7: Make sure all the sides adhere well to the dough.

Step 8: Fold the back side forward to apply even more tension to the dough.

Step 9: Lightly seal the outside with your fingers.

Step 10: Use circular motions to shape the dough into the desired shape.

Step 11: Use circular motions to shape the dough into the desired shape.

Step 12: Use circular motions to shape the dough into the desired shape.

Step 13: Use circular motions to shape the dough into the desired shape.

Step 14: Try not to press too much air out of the dough.

Step 15: There is a lot of tension on the dough and it won't sag.

Step 16: Place the dough in a floured rising basket.

# COLD PROOFING

Now, it's time to let your dough rest for the second, cold fermentation, at about 5–6 °C. This is called the cold proof, second proof, or "second rise," although it's important to keep in mind that your dough isn't actually going to rise more at this stage, certainly not in the fridge– but it will continue to ferment and develop deeper flavors. We are also doing this to stabilize the tension and ensure that your bread keeps its shape; after the cold proof your dough will be firmer and easier to handle when it's time to go into the oven.

There are no hard and fast rules for this second proof: many bakers give their dough 13 hours in the fridge and then straight into the oven, but your dough will be perfectly happy chilling in there even for three days before baking. It's all up to you and your schedule, but this stage is a lifesaver for those who don't have a lot of time to bake, but do love the smell of freshly baking bread in the kitchen every day.

## HANDY RULES OF THUMB

1. To get a bread of the desired size, weigh the dough in advance.
2. Do some stretch and folds by turning the dough over on itself a few times, taking care to push out as little air as possible.
3. Let the dough rest for 10 minutes.
4. Use your dough scraper to help you put your dough in the desired shape.
5. Place it upside down in a floured proofing basket.

## OVER-RISEN DOUGH

Over-risen dough is a common problem; both in artisan bakeries and industrial baking operations. It happens when a dough has passed its optimal fermentation point and the microbial activity, particularly that of the lactic acid bacteria and wild yeasts, has gone on too long. Although fermentation is essential for the development of flavor, structure and digestibility, proofing too long results in loss of structure, collapse of the dough, and an unpleasant acidity that comes from the breakdown of the gluten.

In a properly fermented dough, there is a good balance between gluten formation, gas development and acid production. During fermentation, the microorganisms convert the sugars present into carbon dioxide gas, acids and aromatic compounds. At the same time, proteins and starch structures are slowly being broken down by enzymes, and this makes the dough more supple and easier to work with. However, if this process goes on too long, the gluten network becomes overwhelmed; the acids break down the gluten bonds, gas escapes, and the dough loses its tension. What remains is a saggy, breakable dough that can't keep its shape and will barely rise in the oven, if it rises at all.

An over-risen dough is easy to recognize. It loses its shape and spreads out; its consistency becomes limp and very sticky. It tears easily during shaping, and once you get it into the oven you will generally get a flat bread. The crumb structure will be compact or exhibit irregularly distributed large air pockets. These air pockets are a classic sign of a collapsed gluten network that, after the scoring of the bread, simply had no more tension.

Over-rise is generally due to a combination of factors. The fermentation time and temperature are of crucial importance; at higher temperatures, the microbial activity accelerates dramatically, so it's very easy to overshoot the optimal rise point. High hydration makes the dough more sensitive, because the higher hydration accelerates the breakdown of gluten. Additionally, the quality of the flour plays an important role. Flour with a low protein content or weak gluten strength is less resistant to the acids and enzymes that accumulate during fermentation.

Preventing over-rise depends on proper checking throughout the entire fermentation process. Time, temperature, hydration and flour type must all be factored into the equation. A good core temperature thermometer can be very useful here, but ultimately, the most important thing is observing the dough.

# THE ART OF SCORING

It might seem like an afterthought, but scoring your dough is almost always of vital importance. Not only because it can make or break the oven spring, but because this is where you give your bread your own unique touch. The scoring is where the steam will escape as you bake, and these fault lines will allow the bread to rise evenly. In fact, when you choose where to cut, you are choosing where the bread will rise and what it will look like in the end.

Of course, turning those slices in your dough into a work of art that appears after baking, like you see on some breads from some artisan bakeries, takes a bit of practice. But you might start with a letter or a number (is it somebody's birthday, for example?), and then work up to a name, like some bakeries do.

It's important to remember that not all breads need to be scored: rye bread, for example, contains very little gluten so it's hard to score anyway. With rye bread you get the best and most artisan look by letting the bread rise and crack naturally as it bakes; it will break at the weak spots by itself.

Cakes and confectionery breads like brioches and milk breads don't need to be scored, either; for these, you want to dab a mixture of egg and cream on top before baking, which will give you a smooth and shiny result when it comes out of the oven.

**Scoring your bread helps keep your crumb airy.**

## CHOOSING THE RIGHT KNIFE

A variety of knives will do just fine for scoring your dough; the most important thing is that you use a knife that is razor-sharp, so that you don't pull any dough along when you make your cut. That's why a thinner knife will generally be a better choice than a thick one. Actually, the most commonly used knife for this among sourdough bread bakers is a straight razor (yes, the same one used in the barbershop) with a wooden handle. It's small and maneuverable, so it's easy to make more complicated designs in your dough. In the big bakeries, there's a saying: "a thousand loaves per knife"; but as a home baker you should probably replace your razor blade every month, because they dull fast.

You can also use a serrated bread knife, but with these it's easy to cut too deep.

**Many breads have a classic way of scoring by which you can recognize the bread.**

## SCORING TECHNIQUES

When scoring your dough, there are a number of ways to make the cut depending on the type of dough, the shape of the bread, and the desired end result. It's important to make the cut in one quick and confident motion; if you don't, you will probably drag some dough along with your blade.

- → **Straight cut:** classic and simple, often used on batards or long breads.
- → **Cross cut:** works well on round breads, makes for a rustic look.
- → **"Ear":** a diagonal cut that will make the upper layer of the dough come up as the bread bakes. Popular on baguettes and batards.
- → **Decorative patterns:** primarily for breads with higher water content or rustic boules. With a series of small incisions, the skilled baker creates a pattern, such as leaves or swirls. Aesthetically stunning, but demands practice and timing.

## COMMON MISTAKES

Although the theory behind scoring seems simple, it sometimes goes wrong in practice. Tiny mistakes in timing, technique or tools can have a big impact on the end result. Some of the most common problems, and their potential causes, are listed below:

- → **Dull knife:** your knife drags the dough along with it instead of cutting it cleanly.
- → **No tension in the dough:** you haven't rounded your dough enough, so your cuts don't work as well.
- → **Trying to do too much or too complicated a design:** for beginners, simple is usually best. One or two well-placed cuts are more effective than a complex pattern that disrupts the shape of the bread.
- → **Cutting too deep:** this can make your bread open too far during baking, or even fall apart.
- → **Cutting not deeply enough:** your dough cracks in an uncontrolled manner somewhere you didn't cut, or your cuts are not managing the oven spring.
- → **Holding your knife at the wrong angle:** the angle of the knife is also important for getting a nice oven spring. It's best to hold the knife at a slight angle of 30° while making the cuts.

# THE IMPORTANCE OF MOISTURE DURING BAKING

When properly risen sourdough goes into the oven, it begins its final and perhaps most spectacular phase, as it is transformed from an elastic dough into fragrant, crunchy bread. This transformation is not determined solely by temperature or baking time; an important partner in this equation is also moisture, or perhaps more accurately: steam. Controlling the humidity of the air in your oven, particularly during the first minutes of the baking process, is a fundamental technique that makes the difference between pale, lacklustre bread and a strong, gleaming, perfectly risen result.

## THE ROLE OF STEAM IN THE INITIAL PHASE

As soon as the dough goes into the hot oven, the temperature on its surface shoots up fast. Without steam, that crust would immediately dry out and harden, giving the interior much less space to expand into. Underneath this too rapidly hardened crust, the water remaining in the dough will then, as it heats into steam, have to find its own way out through the weak points in the dough. This can also provide an artisanal look and a nice end result. But thanks to scoring, this moist air comes out quickly and goes straight into the oven, where it keeps the crust from drying out too much for the first 10 minutes. That's exactly enough time for the "oven spring," the phase in which the bread reaches its final volume. The gases in the dough expand, the bread rises, and the scoring on the surface opens up just the way the baker wanted.

→ **Without moisture:** a rigid crust, minimal rise, and generally meagre surface cracking.

→ **With moisture:** an open crumb and the characteristic "ear," the beautiful flap of crumb that opens upward along one side.

### A crispy crust

Without enough steam, bread will often be pale or colour unevenly and have a tough, rubbery crust. That's particularly tragic in the case of sourdough, because then you're missing a big part of what makes the bread so irresistible: the crispy and flavorful crust.

### Tradition and technique

The use of steam is not a modern innovation. In the thick-walled, closed chambers of ancient stone ovens, moisture would hang around a long time. Bakers used wet cloths or poured water on red-hot stones to generate steam artificially. In some traditions, a bundle of straw would be soaked in water and then burned at the mouth of the oven to deliver a quick burst of steam. The methods used are virtually endless, but the goal was always the same: achieving the perfect crust.

### Too much or too little? The search for balance

Just like sourdough itself, here it's all about balance. Too little moisture will keep the bread from rising right and give you an unappealing crust. Too much moisture and you'll get a soft or chewy crust.

## WAYS OF MAKING YOUR OWN STEAM

In a professional bakery, steam injectors can create the right humidity during the baking process at the touch of a button. But few of us have access to such luxuries at home. Fortunately, there are a number of methods available to us, both traditional and effective, to create enough steam in our own home ovens. These techniques bring the bread to life, give us perfectly crispy crusts and allow the bread to rise as it was meant to.

### Baking with a Dutch oven or cast-iron pan

By baking your bread in a preheated cast-iron pan, you can reuse the steam that the bread gives off as it bakes. This is one of the most common methods used by home bakers to get a spectacular end result.

PROCEDURE

→ Heat your oven to the desired temperature with the pan inside.
→ Place your dough on a silicone baking sheet or sheet of baking paper and score it.
→ Put the baking sheet with the dough in the preheated pan and cover with the lid.
→ Remove the lid after one-third of the baking time has passed, to allow the crust to crisp up. Lower the temperature as instructed in the recipe.
→ Continue to bake the bread for the remaining time or until you reach a core temperature of 97 °C.

### Baking in an oven with steam function

Many modern home ovens now have a steam function, and this is essentially identical to the way this is done in a bakery. Setting your oven to the steam function will ensure that you have a suitably moist environment during baking.

PROCEDURE

→ Set your oven to the steam function and preheat to the desired temperature.
→ Place your dough on a silicone baking sheet or sheet of baking paper and score it.
→ Slide it into the oven. When one-third of the baking time has passed, switch from the steam function to the conventional oven with top and bottom heating elements.
→ Lower the temperature as instructed in the recipe.
→ Continue to bake the bread for the remaining time or until you reach a core temperature of 97 °C.

### Baking with a dish of water

This is a simple method that will work in any oven. Use hot water so it evaporates faster and creates the moist environment you need. Always use an oven dish or something that won't break in the heat of the oven.

This is also a good trick if you want your dough to rise faster: Place your dough in a warm oven alongside the dish of water. The water the dish will make sure that your dough doesn't dry out. Just make sure that the oven isn't warmer than 30 °C.

PROCEDURE

→ Preheat your oven to the desired temperature with the dish of hot water in it.
→ Place your dough on a silicone baking sheet or sheet of baking paper and score it.
→ After one-third of the baking time has passed, remove the dish from the oven.
→ Lower the temperature as instructed in the recipe.
→ Continue to bake the bread for the remaining time or until you reach a core temperature of 97 °C.

### Using a spray bottle

If your oven doesn't have a steam function, this alternative is just about as good, and I use it myself a lot. It lets you create a moist environment instantly, and if you need more moisture at any point, just spray again.

PROCEDURE

→ Preheat your oven to the desired temperature.
→ Place your dough on a silicone baking sheet or sheet of baking paper and score it.
→ Use a spray bottle to spray water into the preheated oven for five seconds and then close the oven door.
→ After one-third of the baking time has passed, open the oven door for 10 seconds to allow the steam to escape.

- → Lower the temperature as instructed in the recipe.
- → Continue to bake the bread for the remaining time or until you reach a core temperature of 97 °C.

### Using ice cubes

Putting ice cubes in the preheated oven will create a lot of steam. Just toss them in and that's it! Here again, it's important to not use a glass or ceramic dish, because they can break due to the heat difference.

**PROCEDURE**

- → Preheat your oven to the desired temperature.
- → Place your dough on a silicone baking sheet or sheet of baking paper and score it.
- → Put a dish of ice cubes in the bottom of the oven and close the oven door immediately.
- → After one-third of the baking time has passed, open the oven door for 10 seconds to allow the steam to escape.

- → Lower the temperature as instructed in the recipe.
- → Continue to bake the bread for the remaining time or until you reach a core temperature of 97 °C.

# GRAINS

Gluten behaves differently in different grains because every grain has a different composition of the two major glutinous proteins: gliadin and glutenin. Together, these proteins form the gluten network as soon as they come into contact with water and kneading action. How does gluten behave in the most common grains? See the summary below.

**Wheat**

→ Gluten-rich: high in both gliadin and glutenin.
→ Characteristics: forms a strong, elastic network that retains air. Ideal for bread.
→ Behaviour: good kneading qualities, strong structure.
→ Variants:
→ Soft wheat (for pastries): less gluten, weaker network.
→ Hard wheat/durum: strong but less elastic, better suited for pasta.

**Spelt**

→ Average gluten content, the gluten network is less strong and elastic than wheat.
→ Behaviour: dough is more sensitive, over-kneading will break down the network.
→ Characteristics: somewhat more brittle and more difficult to trap air in; many people find the taste nuttier and lighter.

**Rye**

→ Low gluten: primarily gliadin, almost no glutenin.
→ Behaviour: does not form an elastic network. The dough stays sticky and compact.
→ Solution: for rye bread, fermentation with sourdough is crucial. Enzymes are inhibited, the structure comes more from starch and pentosans (sugars that occur naturally in grains) than from gluten.

| Grain | Gluten? | Type of gluten | Gluten stren |
|---|---|---|---|
| **Wheat** | Yes | Gliadin + glutenin | Strong |
| **Spelt** | Yes | Gliadin + glutenin | Average |
| **Rye** | Little | Secalin | Weak |
| **Kamut** | Yes | Gliadin + glutenin | Average to we |
| **Emmer** | Yes | Gliadin + glutenin | Weak to medi |
| **Einkorn** | Yes | Gliadin + glutenin | Weak |
| **Barley** | Yes | Hordein | Very weak |
| **Oats** | No | None | Very weak |
| **Maize** | No | None | n/a |
| **Buckwheat** | No | None | n/a |

### Kamut (khorasan wheat)

- Contains gluten, but in a different proportion than modern wheat.
- Behaviour: easy to work, but somewhat more brittle than modern wheat. Produces a softer, less airy bread.
- Nutty taste.

### Barley, oats, rice, maize, buckwheat (pseudograins)

- Contain no gluten.
- Behaviour: no network formation → baked product is more crumbly, unless combined with binders or glutinous grains.

| ugh behaviour | Bread structure | Things to note |
|---|---|---|
| astic, kneadable | Airy, rises well | Ideal for classic bread |
| fter, easy to over-knead | More compact | Faster fermentation desirable |
| icky, no network formation | Heavy, solid, compact | Works best with sourdough |
| ky-smooth, less springy | Soft, mild, buttery | Heritage grain, easily digestible |
| ss elastic, easily breakable | Fine, lightly crumbly, compact | Delicate dough, needs a soft touch |
| tremely delicate, fficult to get tension on | Compact, sandy | Very ancient grain, very sensitive to over-kneading |
| gluten network, sticky | Dense, compact, moist | Often malted, good for blending |
| network, crumbly | Soft, dense | Only gluten-free if certified |
| y, crumbly | Compact or cake-like | Good as addition to grain |
| icky, poor binding | Firm, sometimes sandy | Strong, earthy flavor |

# RULE OF THUMB FOR MOST BREAD RECIPES WITH SOURDOUGH

## PROCEDURE

**Day 1 — Evening**
Make the sourdough by taking a bit of starter and feeding it with flour and water.
*The sourdough will rise during the night.*

**Day 2 — Morning**
Autolysis if called for, knead + stretch the dough and fold it using one of the techniques (see *Getting extra tension into the dough,* p. 27).
*Allow bulk fermentation for approximately 4 to 6 hours, until afternoon/evening.*

**Day 2 — Afternoon/evening**
Shape the bread after the bulk fermentation.
*Let it rest 10 minutes.*

**Day 2 — Afternoon/evening**
Shape the dough as desired. Place it in a floured proofing basket or greased baking tin.
If so indicated, rest your dough overnight in the fridge.
*Last cold proof for more flavor.*

**Day 3 — Morning**
Bake the dough at the temperature indicated.

# RECIPES

PASTRY ACADEMY

# I

# BASIC RECIPES

# FARMHOUSE BREAD

An everyday bread made from a mix of wheat and rye. Farmhouse bread contains rye because in bygone days, when wheat was harvested by hand, rye often inadvertently ended up in the wheat.

**DAY 1**
**Ingredients for preparing the sourdough**
10 g sourdough starter
20 g wheat flour
20 g rye flour
40 g water

**DAY 2**
**Ingredients for the mixing bowl**
450 g wheat flour
50 g rye flour
50 g oat flakes
380 g water
13 g salt
90 g risen sourdough from day 1

## PROCEDURE

**DAY 1**
Combine all the ingredients for the sourdough and let rise for 12 hours at room temperature.

**DAY 2**
Place all ingredients in the mixing bowl.
Knead for 4 minutes at low speed and 6 minutes at high speed or until the dough temperature reaches 23 °C. Cover the dough with cling film to prevent it from drying out. Let the dough rest for 10 minutes in the mixing bowl.
Stretch and fold your dough three times, each 30 minutes apart.
Let the bread rise for approximately five hours, until it has nearly doubled in volume.
Shape the dough and place it in a floured proofing basket, covered with a kitchen towel, in the fridge overnight.

**DAY 3**
Place the dough on a baking sheet. Score it in a traditional manner and bake the bread for 15 minutes at 235 °C; lower the heat to 220 °C and bake for a further 30 minutes.
Make sure that you have sufficient steam in the oven during baking (see *The importance of moisture*, p. 39).

# SIMPLE TWISTED BREAD

This is a simple bread you can make even if you haven't mastered shaping a sourdough bread yet. It's quick, but still has a touch of artisanship. A nice addition to a tapas plate or served with soup.

**DAY 1**
**Ingredients for preparing the sourdough**
20 g sourdough starter
40 g wheat flour
40 g water

**DAY 2**
**Ingredients for the mixing bowl**
500 g wheat flour
50 g oat flakes
350 g water
13 g salt
100 g risen sourdough from day 1

## PROCEDURE

**DAY 1**
Combine all the ingredients for the sourdough and let rise for 12 hours at room temperature.

**DAY 2**
Place all the ingredients in the mixing bowl.
Knead for 4 minutes at low speed and 6 minutes at high speed or until the dough temperature reaches 23 °C. Cover the dough with cling film to prevent it from drying out. Let the dough rest for 10 minutes in the mixing bowl.
Stretch and fold the dough once.
Let the bread rise for approximately 5 hours, until it has nearly doubled in volume.
Remove the dough from the bowl and turn it a couple of times.
Place in a floured proofing basket covered with a kitchen towel.
Let it rise for another two hours at room temperature.
Place the dough on a baking sheet. Bake the bread for 15 minutes at 235 °C, reduce heat to 220 °C, and bake for a further 30 minutes.
Make sure that you have sufficient steam in the oven during baking.

# SPELT BREAD

Spelt is the heritage grain from our region. It was being grown here thousands of years ago, and it was long the primary grain in farmhouse bread until wheat made its inroads and pushed spelt out. Nonetheless, spelt remains a beloved grain for its nutty flavor and robust character. Spelt hearkens back to the simplicity and strength of days gone by.

**DAY 1**
**Ingredients for preparing the sourdough**
20 g sourdough starter
20 g wheat flour
20 g spelt flour
40 g water

**DAY 2**
**Ingredients for the mixing bowl**
400 g spelt flour
100 g wheat flour
50 g oat flakes
360 g water
13 g salt
100 g risen sourdough from day 1

## PROCEDURE

**DAY 1**
Combine all the ingredients for the sourdough and let rise for 12 hours at room temperature.

**DAY 2**
Place all the ingredients in the mixing bowl.
Knead for 4 minutes at low speed and 6 minutes at high speed or until the dough temperature reaches 23 °C. Cover the dough with cling film to prevent it from drying out. Let the dough rest for 10 minutes in the mixing bowl.
Stretch and fold your dough three times, each 30 minutes apart.
Let the bread rise for approximately 5 hours, until it has nearly doubled in volume.
Shape the dough and place it in a floured proofing basket, covered with a kitchen towel, in the fridge overnight.

**DAY 3**
Place the dough on a baking sheet. Bake the bread for 15 minutes at 235 °C, lower the temperature to 220 °C, and bake for a further 30 minutes.
Make sure that you have sufficient steam in the oven during baking.

# HAMBURGER BUNS

These hamburger buns are about as far as you can get from fast food. Though they can distantly be traced back to their origins in Hamburg, Germany, Americans adopted and adapted them as a means of making a meal quick and easy to consume. In this sourdough variant they get more flavor, more character, and more long-lasting freshness.

**DAY 1**
**Ingredients for preparing the sourdough**
20 g sourdough starter
40 g wheat flour
40 g water

**DAY 2**
**Ingredients for the mixing bowl**
720 g wheat flour
480 g water
18 g salt
50 g honey
100 g risen sourdough from day 1

**Brush + top with**
1 egg
sesame seeds

## PROCEDURE

**DAY 1**

Combine all the ingredients for the sourdough and let rise at room temperature for 12 hours.

**DAY 2**

Place all ingredients in the bowl of a mixer.
Knead for 4 minutes at low speed and 6 minutes at high speed or until the dough temperature reaches 23 °C. Cover the dough with cling film to prevent it from drying out. Let the dough rest for 10 minutes in the mixing bowl.
Stretch and fold your dough three times, each 30 minutes apart.
Let the bread rise for approximately five hours, until it has nearly doubled in volume.
Divide into portions of 115 g each. Shape into rounds and place them on a baking sheet. Cover them to keep them from drying out and let them rise for another 3 hours.
Brush each round with the beaten egg and sprinkle generously with sesame seeds.
Bake at 200 °C for 20 minutes.
Ensure that there is sufficient steam in the oven during baking.

# SIMPLE WHEAT SOURDOUGH BREAD

This is a good, honest bread that uses nothing other than wheat. Hearty, tasty and rooted in the oldest baking traditions in the world.

**DAY 1**
**Ingredients for preparing the sourdough**
20 g sourdough starter
40 g wheat flour
40 g water

**DAY 2**
**Ingredients for the mixing bowl**
480 g wheat flour
320 g water
13 g salt
100 g risen sourdough from day 1

## PROCEDURE

**DAY 1**
Combine all the ingredients for the sourdough and let rise for 12 hours at room temperature.

**DAY 2**
Place all ingredients in the bowl of a mixer.
Knead for 4 minutes at low speed and 6 minutes at high speed or until the dough temperature reaches 23 °C. Cover the dough with cling film to prevent it from drying out. Let the dough rest for 10 minutes in the mixing bowl.
Stretch and fold your dough three times, each 30 minutes apart.
Let the bread rise for approximately 5 hours, until it has nearly doubled in volume.
Shape the dough and place it in a floured proofing basket covered with a kitchen towel. Let it rest overnight in the fridge.

**DAY 3**
Place the dough on a baking sheet. Bake for 15 minutes at 235 °C; then reduce heat to 220 °C and bake for a further 30 minutes.
Ensure that there is sufficient steam in the oven during baking.

# SOURFAUX BREAD

This faux sourdough, or "sourfaux" if you will, is called that because it presents as true sourdough but is not actually made in the traditional manner with a natural sourdough starter. But don't let the name fool you–it packs all the flavor of a genuine sourdough bread.

**DAY 1**

**Ingredients for preparing the sourdough**

20 g sourdough starter
40 g wheat flour
40 g water

**DAY 2**

**Ingredients for the mixing bowl**

585 g wheat flour
400 g water
13 g salt
4 g dry yeast
100 g risen sourdough from day 1

## PROCEDURE

**DAY 1**

Combine all the ingredients for the sourdough and let rise for 12 hours at room temperature.

**DAY 2**

Place all ingredients in the bowl of a mixer.
Knead for 4 minutes at low speed and 6 minutes at high speed or until the dough temperature reaches 23 °C. Cover the dough with cling film to prevent it from drying out. Let the dough rest for 10 minutes in the mixing bowl.
Stretch and fold your dough three times, each 30 minutes apart.
Let the bread rise for approximately 5 hours, until it has nearly doubled in volume.
Divide the dough in two parts and place it in floured proofing baskets covered with a kitchen towel. Let rest overnight in the fridge.

**DAY 3**

Place the dough on a baking sheet. Bake each loaf for 15 minutes at 235 °C; then reduce heat to 220 °C and bake for a further 30 minutes.
Ensure that there is sufficient steam in the oven during baking.

## VISITING WITH ORGANIC FARMER AND HERITAGE GRAIN EXPERT

# TIJS BOELENS

Along the way on my quest to discover the origin of good bread and the people who are writing its story, I met Tijs Boelens at the Heetveldemolen, a water mill and industrial heritage site in Galmaarden. This meeting was extremely educational for me; although Tijs is not a baker himself, he plays just as critical a role in the process that grain goes through before it ends up in our dough. He is an organic farmer, co-founder of a fantastic vegetable-growing business (De Groentelaar, supplying organic vegetables to Brussels and environs) and, most importantly, an expert in grain agriculture. What he does has a direct impact on the quality and availability of local, healthy flour.

He and his partner at De Groentelaar, Sander Van Haver, grow organic vegetables and grains. But not just any grains–what makes them different is their choice to stick to heritage and seedfast grain species, meaning grains from which you can harvest the seeds to grow new grain: these include einkorn, emmer, spelt, rye, and various heritage strains of wheat. These grains are not selected for maximum yield or processing potential, but for flavor and nutritional value. They work without pesticides or artificial fertilisers, but with careful attention to crop rotation, soil health and biodiversity. Tijs is a firm believer in agro-ecology, an agricultural system that reinforces natural processes and places a high priority on cooperation with fellow farmers, as well as millers, bakers and consumers.

The Heetveldemolen mill is an important partner for Tijs. It's where his grains are stone-ground, in the traditional way, with respect for the product. The miller, Hubert, knows the characteristics of every grain and can adjust his milling process to each. The result is flour that retains more nutrients and offers a richer structure than industrial variants.

This partnership demonstrates how important short supply chains are in the world of sourdough and bread. Thijs sows and harvests, Hubert mills his grain

into flour, and artisan bakers make bread of surpassing quality from it. I see very clearly how every step in the chain has an impact on that quality.

During our conversation, Tijs explained to me how complex and at the same time how essential grain growing is. He talked about the importance of soil structure, timely planning of planting and harvest, and the choice of the grain in service of the goal: bread, beer, pasta or livestock feed. Further, the storage and cleaning of grain also requires a world of knowledge. He pointed out the difference between modern bread-making wheat (with strong gluten) and older grains, which may exhibit shorter gluten formation and so possess exactly the qualities that make them better choices for sourdough and slow fermentation. And heritage strains are often easier to digest, contain more vitamins, and grow well without artificial fertiliser.

What struck me most was his insight into the dependencies within the food chain. "Without bakers actively making the choice for local flour, we wouldn't be able to keep growing our grains," he told me. "And without mills like this one, there would be no one left who could still make a proper product from them at this small scale."

The partnership between Tijs, the mill and the bakers working with their flour is a wonderful example of what is possible when all links in the chain know each other and appreciate their value. As a baker I learned a tremendous amount from Tijs, not only about grain but about how important it is to know our raw materials.

Along with growing grain, Tijs also works to reinforce the local food chain. He delivers his products to local restaurants and shops in Brussels, where they are helping to bridge the gap between farmer and urban consumer. And De Groentelaar also offers vegetable box subscriptions that bring consumers weekly packages of fresh, seasonal vegetables directly from the farm into their homes.

When Tijs took me on a walk through his fields, he told me about what life there is like. As he did, a chorus of meadow birds in the background attested to the fact that it's a good place to be.

# SECOND-CHANCE BREAD

If you ever have too much sourdough and don't know what to do with it, this recipe can help.

**DAY 1**
**Ingredients for the mixing bowl**
480 g wheat flour
315 g water
13 g salt
4 g dry yeast
195 g discard (inactive sourdough starter)

## PROCEDURE

**DAY 1**
Collect your old sourdough starter.
Place all ingredients in the bowl of a mixer.
Knead for 4 minutes at low speed.
Increase speed to high and knead for 6 more minutes, or until the dough reaches a temperature of 23 °C. Cover the dough with cling film to prevent it from drying out. Let the dough rest for 10 minutes in the mixing bowl.
Stretch and fold your dough three times, each 30 minutes apart.
Let rise for approximately two hours, until it has nearly doubled in volume.
Divide the dough into two pieces of 500 g each.
Shape the dough and place it in a floured proofing basket covered with a kitchen towel. Let it rise for a further one hour and 30 minutes at a temperature of 26 °C.
Place the dough on a baking sheet. Score the bread and then bake it for 15 minutes at 235 °C; reduce heat to 220 °C and bake for a further 30 minutes.
Ensure that there is sufficient steam in the oven during baking.

# THREE-GRAIN BREAD

This three-grain bread combines three different heritage grains that have grown on our fields for centuries. Wheat provides the airiness, rye brings a deep, earthy flavor, and spelt adds a nutty note. Together they make a hearty, traditional and nutritious bread.

**DAY 1**
**Ingredients for preparing the sourdough**
20 g sourdough starter
20 g wheat flour
20 g rye flour
40 g water

**DAY 2**
**Ingredients for the mixing bowl**
300 g wheat flour
100 g rye flour
100 g spelt flour
350 g water
13 g salt
100 g risen sourdough from day 1

## PROCEDURE

**DAY 1**
Combine all the ingredients for the sourdough and let rise for 12 hours at room temperature.

**DAY 2**
Place all ingredients in the bowl of a mixer.
Knead for 4 minutes at low speed and 6 minutes at high speed or until the dough temperature reaches 23 °C. Cover the dough with cling film to prevent it from drying out. Let the dough rest for 10 minutes in the mixing bowl.
Stretch and fold your dough three times, each 30 minutes apart.
Let the bread rise for approximately 5 hours, until it has nearly doubled in volume.
Shape the dough and place it in a floured proofing basket covered with a kitchen towel. Let it rest overnight in the fridge.

**DAY 3**
Place the dough on a baking sheet and score it in a traditional manner. Bake for 15 minutes at 235 °C; then lower the heat to 220 °C and bake for a further 30 minutes.
Ensure that there is sufficient steam in the oven during baking.

# HONEY BREAD

Honey gives this bread a warm, lightly sweet flavor and a soft, creamy crumb. In olden times, before sugar was the everyday affordable product we know today, honey was often used as a natural sweetener. This bread is perfect for breakfast or as a comforting snack, a bakery-fresh sweet treat.

**DAY 1**
**Ingredients for preparing the sourdough**
20 g sourdough starter
40 g wheat flour
40 g water

**DAY 2**
**Ingredients for the autolysis**
400 g wheat flour
100 g wholemeal wheat flour
360 g water

**DAY 2**
**Ingredients to add after the autolysis**
60 g honey
13 g salt
100 g risen sourdough from day 1

## PROCEDURE

**DAY 1**
Combine all the ingredients for the sourdough and let rise for 12 hours at room temperature.

**DAY 2**
Place all the ingredients for the autolysis in the bowl of a mixer. Knead for 4 minutes at low speed. Cover the dough with cling film to prevent it from drying out. Perform an autolysis of 30 minutes.
Knead at high speed, adding the honey, salt and risen sourdough, for 6 minutes or until the dough reaches a temperature of 23 °C.
Let the dough rest for 10 minutes in the mixing bowl.
Stretch and fold your dough three times, each 30 minutes apart.
Let the bread rise for approximately 5 hours, until it has nearly doubled in volume.
Shape the dough and place it in a floured proofing basket covered with a kitchen towel. Let it rest overnight in the fridge.

**DAY 3**
Place the dough on a baking sheet and score in a traditional manner. Bake for 15 minutes at 235 °C; reduce heat to 220 °C and bake for a further 30 minutes.
Ensure that there is sufficient steam in the oven during baking.

# LIGHT BROWN BREAD

This bread combines the lightness of wheat flour with the robustness of wheat meal. The result is a light brown crust around a full-flavored, rich crumb that is bursting with flavor thanks to the sourdough fermentation. Perfect for anyone who loves a hearty but easy-to-make bread for every day.

**DAY 1**
**Ingredients for preparing the sourdough**
10 g sourdough starter
20 g wheat flour
20 g rye flour
40 g water

**DAY 2**
**Ingredients for the autolysis**
240 g wheat flour
130 g wheat meal
220 g water

**DAY 2**
**Ingredients to add after the autolysis**
8 g salt
100 g risen sourdough from day 1

## PROCEDURE

**DAY 1**
Combine all the ingredients for the sourdough and let rise for 12 hours at room temperature.

**DAY 2**
Put all the ingredients for the autolysis in the mixing bowl. Knead for 4 minutes at low speed. Cover the dough with cling film to prevent it from drying out. Perform an autolysis of 30 minutes.
Add the salt to the sourdough, then knead at high speed for 6 minutes or until the dough reaches a temperature of 23 °C.
Let the dough rest for 10 minutes in the mixing bowl.
Stretch and fold your dough three times, each 30 minutes apart.
Let the bread rise for approximately five hours, until it has nearly doubled in volume.
Shape the dough and place it in a floured proofing basket covered with a kitchen towel. Let it rest overnight in the fridge.

**DAY 3**
Place the dough on a baking sheet. Score the bread and then bake it for 15 minutes at 235 °C; reduce heat to 220 °C and bake for a further 30 minutes.
Ensure that there is sufficient steam in the oven during baking.

# SANDWICH BREAD

A family favourite that both children and adults find irresistible. With sourdough, every slice has a touch of extra flavor and a lovely open crumb that holds up to a sandwich filling without getting too heavy. The origin of sandwich bread goes back to 18th-century England and is associated with John Montagu, 4th Earl of Sandwich. As the story goes, he was so addicted to card games that he didn't even want to stop to eat, and he would ask his servants to bring him slices of meat between two slices of bread so he could eat with one hand. And so the sandwich was born.

**DAY 1**
**Ingredients for preparing the sourdough**
40 g sourdough starter
80 g wheat flour
80 g water

**DAY 2**
**Ingredients for the mixing bowl**
1100 g wheat flour
590 g water
40 g honey
110 g butter
17 g salt
200 g risen sourdough from day 1

## PROCEDURE

**DAY 1**
Combine all the ingredients for the sourdough and let rise for 12 hours at room temperature.

**DAY 2**
Place all ingredients in the bowl of a mixer.
Knead for 4 minutes at low speed and then at high speed for 8 minutes or until the dough temperature reaches 23 °C.
Cover the dough with cling film to prevent it from drying out.
Let the dough rest for 10 minutes in the mixing bowl.
Stretch and fold your dough three times, each 30 minutes apart.
Let the dough rise for approximately 8 hours, until it has nearly doubled in volume.

**DAY 3**
Divide the dough into two portions of 1000 g each. Shape the dough and place each loaf in a greased bread tin. Let them continue to rise for a further three hours at room temperature and then bake them at 190 °C for 45 minutes.
Ensure that there is sufficient steam in the oven during baking.

## VISITING WITH...

# STÉPHANE VAN CAUWENBERGH

Through Karl De Smedt at the Puratos Sourdough Library, I was introduced to Stéphane Van Cauwenbergh. Karl spoke very highly of him as a baker and a craftsman. Stéphane has an impressive career behind him in the field of baking; he and his wife Lily worked at Puratos for over 25 years, he as technical demonstrator and advisor, travelling throughout Belgium and abroad supporting bakers and development teams working with bread, baked goods and fermentation. After leaving Puratos he and his wife opened their own artisan bakery, Les Pains de Stéphane, where they focus fully on quality, local ingredients, sourdough, and traditional techniques.

Les Pains de Stéphane works with local grains grown barely a mile from the bakery. The flour is stone ground, and Stéphane works it in combination with sourdough cultures he maintains himself, always with slow fermentation; his breads are built up over a period of two to three days. Sourdough fermentation is usually 16 to

20 hours, generally followed by a cold proof of at least 24 hours. This gives his breads a firm structure, longer shelf life and very digestible crumb.

His production is on a small scale. He uses no industrial processes and avoids commercial yeast where possible. His product range consists of various sourdough breads (white, whole-grain, multigrain, spelt, rye) alongside outstanding croissants. He sells his products exclusively in his bakery and occasionally at local events, making the deliberate choice not to sell to wholesalers or dining establishments in order to keep the quality control in his own hands.

When I visited him Stéphane took a great deal of time to show me his processes and answer my questions. He is extremely technically competent, and his years of experience are evident in the precision with which he works. He gave me valuable insights about sourdough care, hydration, flour types and the importance of dough temperature. His working process is straightforward, no-nonsense, technically sound and built around the principle of constant observation of the dough.

I am extremely grateful for his openness and the help he offered me. His knowledge and practical experience have been of substantial value to this book.

# II

# TRADITIONAL BREADS

# WALNUT BREAD

Walnut bread belongs among the traditional breads: rich, filling, and made with ingredients that have been part of the human diet for many centuries. The walnut, with its deep, lightly bitter flavor and healthy fats defines this bread's outspoken character. The combination with sourdough creates a complex, mildly earthy crumb and a crispy crust, with an aroma that brings forest walks and campfires to mind. This is bread as it used to be baked: nutritious, honest and full of life. Heritage grains meet a heritage nut, and together they bring a piece of history to the table.

**DAY 1**
**Ingredients for preparing the sourdough**
20 g sourdough starter
40 g wheat flour
40 g rye flour
80 g water

**DAY 2**
**Ingredients for the autolysis**
365 g wheat flour
145 g rye flour
380 g water
12 g salt
180 g risen sourdough from day 1

**DAY 2**
**Ingredients to add after the autolysis**
50 g walnuts

## PROCEDURE

**DAY 1**

Combine all the ingredients for the sourdough and let rise for 12 hours at room temperature.

**DAY 2**

Put all the ingredients for the autolysis in the mixing bowl. Knead for 4 minutes at low speed. Cover the dough with clingfilm to prevent it from drying out. Perform an autolysis of 20 minutes. At low speed, knead the walnuts into the dough until fully incorporated. Let the dough rest for 10 minutes in the mixing bowl.
Stretch and fold your dough three times, each 30 minutes apart. Let the bread rise for approximately 5 hours, until it has nearly doubled in volume.
Shape the dough and place it in a floured proofing basket covered with a kitchen towel. Let it rest overnight in the fridge.

**DAY 3**

Place the dough on a baking sheet and score. Bake for 15 minutes at 235 °C; then reduce heat to 220 °C and bake for a further 30 minutes.
Ensure that there is sufficient steam in the oven during baking.

# TRADITIONAL KAMUT BREAD

Kamut, also known as khorasan wheat, is an ancient grain with a rich, nutty flavor and a warm yellow-golden colour. Archaeologists have determined that this grain was being grown thousands of years ago across the Fertile Crescent, the sickle-shaped arc stretching across present-day Iran, Iraq, Syria and Egypt. Kamut seeds have been found in Egyptian tombs, which is why it is also sometimes referred to as "the grain of the pharaohs." In this traditional-style bread we combine kamut with emmer, another ancient grain that has been cultivated in the Middle East and the Mediterranean region for thousands of years. Khorasan had been forgotten for centuries until it was rediscovered in the 20$^{th}$ century being cultivated on a small scale in North America.

**DAY 1**
**Ingredients for preparing the sourdough**
35 g sourdough starter
70 g kamut flour
70 g water

**DAY 2**
**Ingredients for the autolysis**
260 g wheat flour
60 g kamut flour
60 g emmer flour
50 g spelt flour
1 g ascorbic acid (optional)
310 g water

**DAY 2**
**Ingredients to add after the autolysis**
100 g germinated sorghum (allowed to sprout and dry again to make the grain sweeter and easier to digest)
10 g salt
175 g risen sourdough from day 1

## PROCEDURE

**DAY 1**
Combine all the ingredients for the sourdough and let rise for 12 hours at room temperature.

**DAY 2**
Put all the ingredients for the autolysis in the mixing bowl. Knead for 2 minutes at low speed. Cover the dough with cling film to prevent it from drying out. Perform an autolysis of 30 minutes.
Knead in the remaining ingredients at high speed for 6 minutes or until the dough reaches a temperature of 23 °C.
Let the dough rest for 10 minutes in the mixing bowl.
Stretch and fold your dough three times, each 30 minutes apart.
Let the bread rise for approximately 5 hours, until it has nearly doubled in volume.
Shape the dough and place it in a floured proofing basket covered with a kitchen towel. Let rest overnight in the fridge.

**DAY 3**
Place the dough on a baking sheet. Score the bread and then bake it for 15 minutes at 235 °C; reduce heat to 220 °C and bake for a further 30 minutes.
Ensure that there is sufficient steam in the oven during baking.

# SEMOLINA BREAD

Semolina, coarsely ground durum wheat, is often associated with pasta, but lends itself perfectly to bread. It makes a crumb that is soft but springy, with a slightly grainy bite and a warm, golden yellow colour that calls to mind the rolling fields of Tuscany. The higher protein content of durum wheat makes this dough somewhat more elastic, but also makes it more difficult to handle, so practice is needed. The bread has a gentle flavor, with a mild wheat taste. It's ideal for dipping in olive oil, serving alongside spiced stews, or simply topping with summery tomato and basil.

**DAY 1**
**Ingredients for preparing the sourdough**
20 g sourdough starter
40 g wheat flour
40 g water

**DAY 2**
**Ingredients for the autolysis**
230 g wheat flour
70 g semolina flour
210 g water

**DAY 2**
**Ingredients to add after the autolysis**
8 g salt
100 g risen sourdough from day 1

## PROCEDURE

**DAY 1**

Combine all the ingredients for the sourdough and let rise for 12 hours at room temperature.

**DAY 2**

Put all the ingredients for the autolysis in the mixing bowl. Knead for 2 minutes at low speed. Cover the dough with clingfilm to prevent it from drying out. Perform an autolysis of 30 minutes.
Knead the other ingredients into the dough at high speed for 6 minutes or until the dough temperature reaches 23 °C.
Let the dough rest for 10 minutes in the mixing bowl.
Stretch and fold your dough three times, each 30 minutes apart.
Let the bread rise for approximately 5 hours, until it has nearly doubled in volume.
Shape the dough and place it in a floured proofing basket covered with a kitchen towel. Let it rest overnight in the fridge.

**DAY 3**

Place the dough on a baking sheet. Score the bread and then bake it for 15 minutes at 235 °C; reduce heat to 220 °C and bake for a further 30 minutes.
Ensure that there is sufficient steam in the oven during baking.

# EINKORN BREAD

Einkorn is one of the oldest types of wheat still grown today and is generally seen as the iconic heritage wheat. Through the centuries, its small, amber grains have always been precious because of the plant's low yield. This grain was already being cultivated 10,000 years ago when the earliest forms of agriculture emerged. Because of the unique composition of the gluten in einkorn, it makes a weaker gluten network than modern wheat, and bread made with it has a softer texture. It is demanding on the baker, but your patience and attention will be rewarded with an extraordinary taste sensation and dazzlingly rustic bread.

**DAY 1**
**Ingredients for preparing the sourdough**
40 g sourdough starter
80 g einkorn flour
80 g water

**DAY 2**
**Ingredients for the autolysis**
540 g einkorn flour
310 g water

**DAY 2**
**Ingredients to add after the autolysis**
10 g salt
200 g risen sourdough from day 1

## PROCEDURE

**DAY 1**
Combine all the ingredients for the sourdough and let rise for 12 hours at room temperature.

**DAY 2**
Put all the ingredients for the autolysis in the mixing bowl. Knead for 2 minutes at low speed. Cover the dough with clingfilm to prevent it from drying out. Perform an autolysis of 30 minutes.
Knead the other ingredients into the dough at high speed for 4 minutes or until the dough temperature reaches 23 °C. Einkorn is sensitive to over-kneading.
Let the dough rest for 10 minutes in the mixing bowl.
Stretch and fold your dough three times, each 30 minutes apart.
Let the dough rise for approximately 5 hours, until it has expanded by approximately 30% in volume.
Shape the dough and place it in a floured proofing basket covered with a kitchen towel. Let it rest overnight in the fridge.

**DAY 3**
Place the dough on a baking sheet. Score the bread and then bake it for 15 minutes at 235 °C; reduce heat to 220 °C and bake for a further 30 minutes. Ensure that there is sufficient steam in the oven during baking.

# PITA BREAD

Pita bread is one of the oldest forms of bread in the world. It originated in the region around Egypt some time around 3000 BC. Its characteristic air bubbles are formed by the high temperature at which the bread is baked, which converts the water in the dough into steam very quickly and makes it "blow up" like a balloon.

**DAY 1**
**Ingredients for preparing the sourdough**
30 g sourdough starter
60 g wheat flour
60 g water

**DAY 2**
**Ingredients for the mixing bowl**
1000 g wheat flour
600 g water
22 g salt
5 g baker's yeast
150 g risen sourdough from day 1

**DAY 2**
**Ingredients for the bassinage**
110 g water
60 g olive oil

## PROCEDURE

**DAY 1**
Combine all the ingredients for the sourdough and let rise for 12 hours at room temperature.

**DAY 2**
Combine all the ingredients in the bowl of a mixer and knead for 4 minutes at low speed and 7 minutes at high speed. Add the water and olive oil for the bassinage. Cover the dough with cling film to prevent it from drying out.
Stretch and fold the dough once.
Transfer to the fridge and leave overnight.

**DAY 3**
Remove the dough from the fridge. Divide into 19 pieces of 100 g each and shape them into rounds. Let rise for two hours at room temperature. Punch down and roll each ball out into a circle 16 cm in diameter. Bake them at 280 °C for 4 minutes.

# RUSTIC HEARTH BREAD

The name of this bread is derived from the French *pavé rustique*. Its origin goes back to the 18th-century countryside bakeries where bread was often baked in wood-fired ovens with no baking tin or mould.

**DAY 1**
**Ingredients for the preparation of the stiff sourdough**
110 g sourdough starter
110 g wheat flour
60 g water

**DAY 2**
**Ingredients for the mixing bowl**
450 g wheat flour
50 g rye flour
350 g water
13 g salt
280 g risen stiff sourdough

**DAY 2**
**Ingredients for the bassinage**
90 g water

## PROCEDURE

**DAY 1**
With the dough hook, knead all the ingredients for the stiff sourdough and let rise for 12 hours at room temperature.

**DAY 2**
Place all ingredients in the bowl of a mixer.
Knead for 4 minutes at low speed and 6 minutes at high speed or until the dough reaches 23 °C. Cover the dough with cling film to prevent it from drying out.
Let the dough rest for 10 minutes in the mixing bowl.
Add the water for the bassinage and stretch and fold it into your dough. Stretch and fold your dough three times, each 30 minutes apart.
Let the bread rise for approximately five hours, until it has nearly doubled in volume.
Carefully divide your dough into two pieces of 610 g each.
Place them on a baking sheet without shaping them. Let them rise for two hours and then score them. Bake at 240 °C for 20 minutes; then lower the heat to 220 °C and bake for another 20 minutes.

# HAZELNUT TIGER BREAD

What could be tastier than a compact sourdough roll bursting with zesty, flavorful nuts? This recipe does require some practice to get a visually appealing end result, but your guests will be speechless when they taste this timeless classic.

**DAY 1**
**Ingredients for preparing the sourdough**
30 g sourdough starter
60 g wheat flour
60 g water

**DAY 2**
**Ingredients for the mixing bowl**
450 g wheat flour
50 g rye flour
350 g water
10 g salt
150 g risen sourdough from day 1

**DAY 2**
**Ingredients for the tiger mix**
100 g rye flour
150 g dark beer
4 g salt
3 g baker's yeast

**Addition**
200 g hazelnuts

## PROCEDURE

**DAY 1**

Combine all the ingredients for the sourdough and let rise for 12 hours at room temperature.

**DAY 2**

Roast the hazelnuts in a 150 °C oven for 15 minutes. Chop them coarsely and set aside.
Place all ingredients in the bowl of a mixer.
Knead for 4 minutes at low speed and 6 minutes at high speed or until the dough temperature reaches 23 °C. Cover the dough with cling film to prevent it from drying out.
Let your dough rest in the mixing bowl for 20 minutes.
Add the chopped nuts and stretch and fold them into your dough.
Stretch and fold again 30 minutes later, and repeat 30 minutes later. Let the bread rise for approximately five hours, until it has nearly doubled in volume.
Divide the dough into three pieces of 350 g each. Shape them and place each one in a floured proofing basket. Cover with a kitchen towel.

**DAY 3**

Combine the ingredients for the tiger mix and let ferment for 1 hour.
Transfer the dough to a baking sheet. Spread the tiger mix over each and bake at 250 °C for 30 minutes.
Ensure that there is sufficient steam in the oven during baking.

# FERMENTERRY

This combination of sweet honey, blueberries and sourdough delivers an absolutely unique flavor explosion to your breakfast table. For a true original, try replacing some of the water with berry juice.

**DAY 1**
**Ingredients for preparing the sourdough**
20 g sourdough starter
40 g rye flour
40 g water

**DAY 2**
**Ingredients for the mixing bowl**
470 g wheat flour
30 g rye flour
350 g water
13 g salt
15 g honey
10 g sugar
15 g butter
5 g ground cinnamon
100 g risen sourdough from day 1

**Addition**
200 g blueberries

## PROCEDURE

**DAY 1**
Combine all the ingredients for the sourdough and let rise for 12 hours at room temperature.

**DAY 2**
Place all ingredients in the bowl of a mixer.
Knead for 4 minutes at low speed and 6 minutes at high speed or until the dough temperature reaches 23 °C. Cover the dough with cling film to prevent it from drying out. Add the blueberries and mix for one minute at low speed.
Let the dough rest for 10 minutes in the mixing bowl.
Stretch and fold your dough three times, each 30 minutes apart.
Let the bread rise for approximately 5 hours, until it has nearly doubled in volume.
Shape the dough and place it in a floured proofing basket covered with a kitchen towel. Let it rest overnight in the fridge.

**DAY 3**
Place the dough on a baking sheet and score it in a traditional manner. Bake for 15 minutes at 235 °C; then reduce heat to 220 °C and bake for a further 30 minutes.
Ensure that there is sufficient steam in the oven during baking.

# PANIS QUADRATUS

This is a modern variation on the Roman bread that archaeologists found at Pompeii. The remains of the charred and completely carbonised bread found there were dated back to the first century BC. To give this bread its characteristic shape, the ancient Romans used string to hold the dough together.

**DAY 1**
**Ingredients for preparing the sourdough**
20 g sourdough starter
40 g rye flour
40 g water

**DAY 2**
**Ingredients for the mixing bowl**
300 g spelt flour
200 g wholemeal spelt flour
350 g water
10 g salt
100 g risen sourdough from day 1

## PROCEDURE

**DAY 1**
Combine all the ingredients for the sourdough and let rise for 12 hours at room temperature.

**DAY 2**
Place all ingredients in the bowl of a mixer.
Knead for 4 minutes at low speed and 6 minutes at high speed.
Cover the dough with cling film to prevent it from drying out.
Let the dough rest for 10 minutes in the mixing bowl.
Stretch and fold your dough three times, each 30 minutes apart.
Let the bread rise for approximately 5 hours, until it has nearly doubled in volume.
Shape the dough and tie three strings around the dough at equally spaced intervals. Place the dough on a baking sheet.
Continue to let it rise for another 2 hours.
Bake for 15 minutes at 235 °C; then reduce heat to 220 °C and bake for a further 30 minutes.
Ensure that there is sufficient steam in the oven during baking.

## VISITING WITH...

# HEETVELDMOLEN

In the tranquil countryside west of Brussels, where the morning mist lingers long over the fields and the River Mark is lined with pollarded willows, you will find the Heetveldemolen: an old water mill with a wooden wheel and a stone heart. Here they still mill flour the way they used to: with attention, time and running water.

When I arrived there, Hubert, the miller, was already waiting for me in his work shirt. The air was thick with the scent of freshly ground flour: warm, nutty, almost herbal. "Come in," he said in a low, calming voice.

He accompanied me inside past sacks of heritage grain to the rhythmic creaking of giant gears. His hands spoke of craftsmanship. This mill is his world. As well as his wife Monique's: it was her family that bought the mill, once upon a time, driven by the will to preserve something that otherwise would have been lost. What started out as a restoration project became a life project.

Today, she and her husband continue that work. Together they are a couple that not only manages the mill, but also embodies a way of life: slow, honest, rooted in ground and grain.

The mill grinds slowly, powered by the river. Stone-ground flour leaves the building without having lost germ, bran, or character. "The grain tells you what it needs," Hubert said, inspecting a handful of spelt flour. "And we listen."

Wheat, spelt, emmer, einkorn, even kamut: what this mill grinds is heritage grains from local farmers. The result: flour with aroma, texture, and life-miles away from the factory flour most people know. I could

feel the difference just by touching it. For sourdough bakers, this is not an ingredient; it's a partner.

What struck me is the rhythm. Everything there happens at the tempo of water, wind and season. No clock that forces, no production that pushes. Hubert and Monique work with respect for the mill, for each type of grain, and for the traditional cycle in which nothing needs to be, and in which nothing can be, hastened.

Hubert showed me how the grain, sourced from local farmers, is hoisted up and then slowly fed into the millstones–shaped with precision by Hubert and Dirk themselves–that grind the grain, without heating or crushing it.

"That's how you keep the natural enzymes, the germ, the bran, intact," Hubert explained to me. "Our flour is living flour, and you can taste it."

The mill grinds grains that are thousands of years old and are coming back into the spotlight. With each, Hubert knows what he's doing: every grain demands its own setting and its own attention. "You can't just force everything down through the same stones. Every grain has its own character." For anyone who works with sourdough, this flour is worth its weight in gold. It still has all the nutrients from the grain, ready for fermentation.

The bread that we took out of the oven was compact, crispy, and full of character, just like the place itself. Pure, honest bread, grown right here, miles away from the fluffy white bread in the supermarkets of Brussels. And so the cycle goes: the farmer who sows, the miller who mills, the baker who kneads, the man who eats. Each their own craft, all in their own time.

ELT
organic

# III

# SWEET SOURDOUGH

# SOURDOUGH BANANA BREAD

This delicious little recipe is my own upgrade to the banana bread recipe I picked up during my studies in Las Vegas. The sourdough adds a subtle edge that does the sweetness of the banana bread good. It's much more balanced than a typical sweet banana bread. As always, the blacker the bananas you use, the better.

**DAY 1**

**Ingredients for the mixing bowl**

210 g overripe bananas
2.6 g salt
2.6 g baking soda
200 g sugar
100 g neutral oil
100 g eggs
150 g wheat flour
160 g active sourdough or discard (inactive sourdough)
1 vanilla pod

**Topping**

chopped walnuts

## PROCEDURE

**DAY 1**

Preheat the oven to 180 °C.

Combine the baking soda, salt and wheat flour in a bowl and set aside.

In the bowl of a mixer, mix the bananas with the sugar and sourdough for 4 minutes at high speed. Add the eggs and mix for 2 minutes more at high speed until the eggs are incorporated.

Reduce the speed to medium and gradually add the baking soda, salt and wheat flour mix (approximately 1/3 at a time) to the bananas. When the dry ingredients are incorporated, add the neutral oil and continue to mix for another 2 minutes.

Transfer the batter into a greased baking tin and sprinkle with walnuts. Bake at 180 °C for 40 minutes or until done.

# "SANDWICHES"

Be careful in Belgium, because "sandwich" might refer not to a sandwich as you know it, but to these light and fluffy buns. A beloved fixture at Belgian bakeries and cafés, they also appear like magic at every family gathering. Making them with sourdough gives them a subtle depth without conflicting with their refined sweetness. Ideal with jam, baked ham, or simply enjoyed plain for breakfast or at brunch.

**DAY 1**

**Ingredients for preparing the sourdough**

50 g sourdough starter
100 g wheat flour
100 g warm, full-fat milk

**DAY 2**

**Ingredients for the mixing bowl**

900 g wheat flour
400 g warm milk
100 g eggs
10 g baker's yeast
40 g sugar
150 g butter (min. 82% fat)
15 g salt
250 g risen sourdough from day 1

**To brush**

1 egg

## PROCEDURE

**DAY 1**

Combine all the ingredients for the sourdough and let rise for 12 hours at room temperature.

**DAY 2**

Place all ingredients in the bowl of a mixer.
Knead for 4 minutes at low speed and 4 minutes at high speed or until the dough temperature reaches 23 °C. Cover the dough with cling film to prevent it from drying out.
Let your dough rest for 10 minutes in the bowl, then stretch and fold the dough once.
Let rise for 2 hours until the dough has nearly doubled in volume. Divide into pieces of 75 g each. Shape the dough by taking a piece of dough and laying your hands around it with your fingernails flat on the work surface. Round each piece and let rest for 10 minutes.
Punch down and then roll the sandwiches. Place them on a baking sheet, covered to prevent them from drying out, and let rise for one and a half hours. Brush with the beaten egg and bake at 230 °C for 10 minutes.

# SOURDOUGH BRIOCHE

Brioche is a French bread; specifically, its roots can be traced back to Normandy, a region famous for its butter. The name of the bread may come from Old French *brier*, meaning "to knead." Originally it was a bread for festive occasions, a symbol of wealth (in consideration of how much butter goes into it, not to mention the eggs); but since then brioche has earned its place in the greater pantheon of French baking culture. In this version, sourdough makes for a slower fermentation process and a deep, layered flavor that the luxurious dough only elevates.

**DAY 1**
**Ingredients for preparing the sourdough**
10 g sourdough starter
20 g wheat flour
20 g milk

**DAY 2**
**Ingredients for the preparation of the pre-ferment**
120 g wheat flour
120 g milk (35 °C)
50 g risen sourdough
12 g granulated sugar

**DAY 2**
**Ingredients for the mixing bowl**
400 g wheat flour
25 g granulated sugar
8 g salt
200 g eggs
160 g softened butter
302 g pre-ferment

**To brush**
1 egg

## PROCEDURE

**DAY 1**
Combine all the ingredients for the sourdough and let rise for 12 hours at room temperature.

**DAY 2**
In a bowl, combine all the ingredients for the pre-ferment and let rise for 4 hours at 23 °C.

**DAY 2**
Place all ingredients in the bowl of a mixer.
Knead for 4 minutes at low speed and 10 minutes at high speed or until the dough temperature reaches 23 °C. Cover the dough with cling film to prevent it from drying out.
Let the dough rest for 10 minutes in the mixing bowl.
Stretch and fold your dough three times, each 30 minutes apart.
Let the dough rise for approximately 5 hours until it has nearly doubled in volume.
Divide the dough into eight pieces of 135 g each. Round them.
Transfer the rounds into a greased baking tin. Let them rise for another 4–6 hours.
Brush with a beaten egg.
Bake the brioche at 230 °C for 30 minutes.

# CINNAMON ROLLS

Cinnamon rolls like these are beloved throughout Scandinavia, and every bakery has its own unique recipe. The natural fermentation deepens the flavor and brings out the sweet cinnamon-spice aroma even better. A word of warning: the winter-wonderland smell can linger in your kitchen for days, reminding you of the heavenly flavor.

**DAY 1**

**Ingredients for preparing the sourdough**

40 g sourdough starter
80 g wheat flour
80 g milk

**DAY 2**

**Ingredients for the mixing bowl**

500 g strong white bread flour
140 g milk (35 °C)
200 g eggs
55 g granulated sugar
12 g salt
200 g risen sourdough
200 g butter at room temperature

**To brush**

1 egg

**DAY 3**

**Ingredients for the filling**

500 g cream cheese (such as Philadelphia)
75 g powdered sugar
50 g condensed milk
40 g ground cinnamon

## PROCEDURE

**DAY 1**

Combine all the ingredients for the sourdough and let rise for 12 hours at room temperature.

**DAY 2**

In the mixing bowl, knead the flour, milk, eggs, sugar and salt in the mixing bowl at high speed for 11 minutes. Gradually add the butter and then knead for 3 more minutes until all the butter is incorporated. Cover the dough with cling film to prevent it from drying out.
Let the dough rest for 10 minutes in the mixing bowl.
Stretch and fold your dough three times, each 30 minutes apart.
Let the dough rise for approximately 5 hours until it has nearly doubled in volume. Transfer to the fridge overnight.

**DAY 3**

Roll the cold dough out on a floured work surface into a rectangle of 28 x 55 cm.
In a bowl, combine the filling ingredients, beat until smooth, and then spread over the top of the dough rectangle with a spatula, completely covering the dough. Roll the dough up, beginning from the long side. Using a sharp knife, cut 4 cm pieces from the roll and place them on a baking sheet.
Let them rise for another 2 hours in a warm place (25 °C).
Brush each roll with a beaten egg.
Bake the cinnamon rolls at 200 °C for 20–25 minutes.

# ENGLISH MUFFINS

Soft on the inside, lightly crunchy on the outside and full of tiny little holes: English muffins have been a permanent fixture on British breakfast tables since at least the 18th century. Originally cooked on cast-iron plates over an open fire, they were popularized as street food in Victorian England. In this version, sourdough provides a light acidity without making any concessions on their characteristic texture.

**DAY 1**
**Ingredients for the preparation of the sourdough**
20 g sourdough starter
40 g wheat flour
40 g water

**DAY 2**
**Ingredients for the mixing bowl**
360 g strong white bread flour
20 g honey
240 g milk
5 g salt
100 g risen sourdough

**To sift, for baking**
40 g corn flour

## PROCEDURE

**DAY 1**
Combine all the ingredients for the sourdough and let rise for 12 hours at room temperature.

**DAY 2**
Place all ingredients in the bowl of a mixer.
Knead for 4 minutes at low speed and 7 minutes at high speed.
Cover the dough with cling film to prevent it from drying out.
Let the dough rest in the bowl for 40 minutes. Stretch and fold your dough three times, each 30 minutes apart.
Let the dough rise for 8 hours until it has nearly doubled in volume. Place the dough on a floured work surface and divide into pieces of 100 g per muffin. Round them and then press them flat with the palm of your hand to a thickness of 1 cm. Cover them to keep them from drying out and let rise for two hours. Sift a little cornmeal over the muffins. Fry the muffins for 5 minutes on each side in a preheated pan low heat.

# SOURDOUGH PANCAKES

These pancakes are an ideal way to use up leftover sourdough. Somebody wants pancakes? Like magic, in less than five minutes you're serving them up.

**Ingredients for the mixing bowl**
125 g wheat flour
200 g eggs
250 g milk
3 g salt
50 g sugar
20 g melted butter
60 g active sourdough or discard (inactive sourdough)
5 g vanilla paste or 1 vanilla bean

## PROCEDURE

Place all ingredients in a mixing bowl.
Whisk everything together until you have a smooth batter.
Melt a pat of butter in a preheated pan and fry the pancakes until golden brown.

# SOFT BUTTER ROLLS

Straight from the oven, with a crust so thin it cracks under your fingers. These butter rolls take their time rising thanks to the sourdough, which also gives them their full, well-rounded flavor. They're awfully close to the pistolets you might get from your favorite French bakery.

**DAY 1**
**Ingredients for preparing the sourdough**
40 g sourdough starter
40 g wheat flour
40 g water

**DAY 2**
**Ingredients for the mixing bowl**
500 g wheat flour
270 g water
10 g honey
45 g butter
13 g salt
120 g risen sourdough from day 1

## PROCEDURE

**DAY 1**
Combine all the ingredients for the sourdough and let it rise for 12 hours at room temperature.

**DAY 2**
Place all ingredients in the bowl of a mixer.
Knead for 4 minutes at low speed and 6 minutes at high speed or until the dough temperature reaches 23 °C. Cover the dough with cling film to prevent it from drying out. Let the dough rest for 10 minutes in the mixing bowl.
Stretch and fold your dough three times, each 30 minutes apart.
Let the dough rise for approximately 6 hours until it has nearly doubled in volume.
Divide the dough into seven pieces of 140 g each. Round them and place them on a baking sheet. Set aside in the fridge overnight.

**DAY 3**
Let the rolls rise at room temperature for four hours until they have nearly doubled in size. Bake them at 190 °C for 20 minutes until golden brown.
Ensure there is sufficient steam in the oven during baking.

# CHOCOLATE COOKIES

These chocolate cookies combine the deep, rich flavor of dark chocolate with the subtle complexity of sourdough. The natural fermentation gives the dough a light acidity that perfectly balances the sweetness, interspersed with flavor explosions from the dark chocolate bits. Crispy on the outside and gooey on the inside, irresistible for any coffee break.

**Ingredients for the mixing bowl**
380 g wheat flour
220 g butter
5 g baking powder
5 g baking soda
5 g salt
210 g granulated sugar
220 g brown sugar
45 g egg yolk
500 g dark chocolate, coarsely chopped
1 vanilla bean or 5 g vanilla paste
230 g active sourdough or discard (inactive sourdough)

## PROCEDURE

Make *beurre noisette* (brown butter) by heating the butter in a pan for a few minutes, until all the bubbles have disappeared (these are the proteins). This is important not only for the flavor, but to cook off the water in the butter. Pour this hot butter into the bowl of a mixer. Add the sugar and mix with the K beater attachment at high speed for 2 minutes. Add the sourdough and the egg yolk and mix at medium speed for another 2 minutes until you have a coarse mass. Add the remaining dry ingredients and mix for 10 seconds at low speed until your flour mixture begins to come together with your butter mixture, and then add the chocolate. Beat for one more minute at medium speed until all the chocolate is incorporated. Cover the dough with cling film to keep it from drying out.

For best results, put the mixing bowl in the fridge and let stand for 3–12 hours.

Break off a 70 g piece of dough for each cookie and roll into balls by hand. Arrange the balls on the baking sheet.

Bake at 180 °C for 18 minutes.

# LIÈGE WAFFLES

Not to be confused with Belgian waffles, this style of waffle originated in Liège at the end of the 19th century. They differ in their dense, brioche-like dough and the addition of pearl sugar, which caramelises while cooking and turns into the irresistibly sweet, crunchy crust. Originally a simple food for the masses, today they are loved around the world as authentic Belgian street food.

**DAY 1**
**Ingredients for preparing the sourdough**
30 g sourdough starter
60 g wheat flour
60 g water

**DAY 2**
**Ingredients for the mixing bowl**
250 g wheat meal
5 g salt
20 g granulated sugar
120 g butter, softened
50 g milk
50 g egg
150 g risen sourdough from day 1

**DAY 2**
**Ingredients to add after resting**
120 g pearl sugar

## PROCEDURE

**DAY 1**
Combine all the ingredients for the sourdough and let rise for 12 hours at room temperature.

**DAY 2**
In the bowl of a mixer, combine the milk, egg and sourdough.
Beat at high speed for 2 minutes.
In a separate bowl, combine the dry ingredients and add them along with the butter to the batter in the bowl of the mixer.
Switch the beater for the dough hook and knead for 4 minutes at low speed and 6 minutes at high speed until you have full gluten development. Cover the dough with cling film to keep it from drying out. Stretch and fold your dough once.
Let the dough rest in the bowl for 3 hours.
Punch down and knead the pearl sugar through the dough until it is evenly distributed.
Divide the dough into pieces of 100 g each. Fry them in a Liège waffle iron at 180 °C for 3 minutes.

# DESSERT MUFFINS

The reason dessert muffins are so popular is that they are so easy to make. By using yogurt with a lemon, you get an exciting, slightly acidic end result. The perfect surprise to cap off a successful dinner party with your guests.

**Ingredients for the mixing bowl**
210 g wheat flour
zest of 2 lemons
160 g granulated sugar
55 g brown sugar
3 g salt
10 g baking powder
15 g poppyseed
100 g eggs
125 g yoghurt
110 g butter
115 g active sourdough or discard (inactive sourdough)

**Lemon glaze**
100 g powdered sugar
juice of 2 lemons

## PROCEDURE

Combine all the dry ingredients and set them aside.
Melt the butter over low heat.
In another bowl whisk the eggs, yogurt and sourdough together until you have a smooth batter; fold in the melted butter.
With a spatula, fold the dry ingredients into the batter until no flower remains at the bottom of the bowl and all clumps are dissolved. Cover with cling film to prevent the dough from drying out and leave to rise in the fridge for 2 hours.
Fill each muffin form to two-thirds full.
Bake at 200 °C for 25 minutes.
For the lemon glaze, combine the powdered sugar with the lemon juice. Let the muffins cool and then spoon the glaze over the muffins.

# JAM COOKIES

You find them in every shop: little sandwiches of dry cookies with jam in the middle. After you make this recipe, they will probably be a permanent fixture in your pantry. Fill them with homemade summer jams. Sweet and fruity, with a light acidity from the sourdough, they are a perfect way to use your sourdough.

**DAY 1**
**Ingredients for the mixing bowl**
310 g wheat flour
150 g almond flour
3 g salt
4 g cinnamon
350 g butter
200 g granulated sugar
1 vanilla bean or 5 g vanilla paste
1 egg yolk
110 g active sourdough or discard (inactive sourdough)

**Addition**
your choice of jam

## PROCEDURE

**DAY 1**
In a bowl combine the flour, almond flour, salt, and cinnamon and set aside.
With the K beater attachment, beat the butter and the sugar for two minutes at high speed until creamy and light. Do not over-beat or the butter will split. Add the vanilla, the egg yolk and the sourdough and continue to beat at high speed until you have a fluffy batter.
Gradually add the dry ingredients while continuing to beat at low speed. Stop immediately when the ingredients are incorporated. Wrap in cling film and set aside in the fridge for at least 4–12 hours. This dough can be stored in the fridge for up to a week.

**DAY 2**
On a floured work surface, roll out the dough to a thickness of 3 mm. Cut out the cookies with a round cutter. Collect the trimmings and set them back in the fridge to use next time.
Bake the cookies in a 170 °C oven for 14 minutes.
When the cookies are cooled, take one and spread some jam on the top. Top that with another cookie.
For a beautiful end result, dust with powdered sugar on top of the cookies.

# ITALIAN LEMON CAKE

This tangy and light lemon cake brings the Italian sun straight to your plate. The puckery combination of fresh lemons and limoncello is a beloved dessert in many Italian regions, particularly in spring and summer. The addition of sourdough gives the cake a light, natural acidity that accentuates the citrus flavors. A perfect closer to a meal or light bite to accompany an espresso.

**DAY 1**

**Ingredients for preparing the sourdough**

20 g sourdough starter
40 g wheat flour
40 g water

**DAY 2**

**Ingredients for the mixing bowl**

180 g neutral oil
430 g wheat flour
8 g baking powder
3 g salt
zest of 1 lemon
230 g granulated sugar
200 g eggs
200 g milk
25 g limoncello
5 g vanilla paste or 1 vanilla bean
100 g risen sourdough from day 1

## PROCEDURE

**DAY 1**

Combine all the ingredients for the sourdough and let it rise for 12 hours at room temperature.

**DAY 2**

In a bowl, combine the flour, baking powder, salt and lemon zest. Set aside.

Beat the eggs and sugar at high speed for 3 minutes until thick and pale yellow. Add the milk, limoncello, oil, vanilla and sourdough and beat for another 2 minutes. Fold in the dry ingredients with a spatula and stir until smooth. Pour into a greased baking tin and bake at 180 °C for 45 minutes.

# NORWEGIAN BOLLER

You can't be a baker in Norway without having this recipe in your repertoire. A Scandinavian variation on brioche, these light and fluffy sweet buns are made by the truckload in Norway every day, and everyone loves them. If you want them sweeter, try a variant with chocolate or berries.

**DAY 1**
**Ingredients for preparing the sourdough**
30 g sourdough starter
40 g wheat flour
40 g water

**DAY 2**
**Ingredients for the mixing bowl**
650 g wheat flour
340 g milk
100 g eggs
200 g sugar
5 g salt
120 g butter
10 g cardamom
110 g risen sourdough from day 1

**To brush**
1 egg

## PROCEDURE

**DAY 1**
Combine all the ingredients for the sourdough and let rise for 12 hours at room temperature.

**DAY 2**
Place all ingredients in the bowl of a mixer. Knead for 4 minutes at low speed and 6 minutes at high speed. Cover the dough with cling film to prevent it from drying out. Let the dough rest for 10 minutes in the mixing bowl.
Stretch and fold your dough three times, each 30 minutes apart. Let the dough rise for around 7 hours, until it has nearly doubled in volume.
Set aside in the fridge overnight.

**DAY 3**
Divide the dough into 15 pieces of 100 g each and shape them into rounds. Place each around on a baking sheet, cover them to prevent them from drying out and let rise for another 8 hours. Brush with a beaten egg and bake at 230 °C for 10 minutes.

# BROWNIES

Brownies are a classic, perhaps the classic, American baked good. They've been around since the early 20th century, and their creamy interior surrounded by a delicate dark chocolate crust has made them beloved ever since. In this version sourdough not only achieves that picture-perfect soft texture but adds a subtle depth and complexity to the intense chocolate flavor. The slightly acidic note of the natural fermentation is the perfect balance for the sweet. Rich, dark and intriguingly different, these are brownies for people who are looking for something far from average.

**Ingredients for the mixing bowl**
120 g butter
280 g pure chocolate
40 g cacaopoeder
5 g vanilla paste or marrow of 1 vanilla bean
100 g eggs
240 g granulated sugar
115 g brown sugar
90 g wheat flour
5 g salt
125 g active sourdough or discard (inactive sourdough)

## PROCEDURE

In a pan on low heat, melt the butter with the vanilla.
Stir the chocolate into this mixture until it is completely melted.
Combine all dry ingredients in a separate bowl.
Mix the butter mixture into the bowl until smooth.
Add the eggs and sourdough starter and stir well again.
Pour the batter onto a baking sheet lined with baking paper.
Bake the brownies at 180 °C for 40 minutes.

# BREAD PUDDING

Bread pudding is a venerable classic country recipe. But when you use old sourdough bread, it takes on a new life. The firm crust will absorb the custard (the mixture of milk, eggs and sugar) very well and add a lovely bitter note to the sweetness. Against the harmonies of raisins and cinnamon, it is an ode to simplicity and the philosophy of zero waste.

**Ingredients for the mixing bowl**
1000 g full-fat milk
200 g brown sugar
200 g white sugar
600 g old sourdough bread or sweet baked goods
400 g raisins
500 g eggs
50 g butter
1 g cinnamon
5 g vanilla paste (or seeds of 1 vanilla bean)

## PROCEDURE

Heat the milk with the sugar until melted.
Break the bread into small pieces and immerse them in the milk.
Leave them a few minutes to soak.
Add the rest of the ingredients and stir.
Transfer to a greased baking tin and bake at 200 °C for 40 minutes.

IV

# INTER-NATIONAL RECIPIES

# SOURDOUGH PIZZA

In this recipe, the sourdough-based pizza crust has been given time to ripen, and you will taste it in every bite. The natural fermentation makes for a crispy crust, an airy interior, and a deeper flavor. If you're looking for artisinal, simple and pure, look no further.

**DAY 1**
**Ingredients for preparing the sourdough**
200 g sourdough starter
200 g wheat flour
200 g water

**DAY 2**
**Ingredients for the mixing bowl**
2000 g t00 pizza flour
1350 g water
72 g salt
splash of olive oil
600 g risen sourdough from day 1

## PROCEDURE

**DAY 1**
Combine all the ingredients for the sourdough and let rise for 12 hours at room temperature.

**DAY 2**
Knead the water and flour for 2 minutes. Cover the dough with cling film to prevent it from drying out. Perform an autolysis of 30 minutes.
Add the sourdough, the salt, and the olive oil. Knead at high speed for 8 minutes or until the dough reaches a temperature of 23 °C. Cover the dough with cling film to prevent it from drying out. Let the dough rest for 10 minutes in the mixing bowl.
Stretch and fold your dough once.
Let it rest overnight in the fridge.

**DAY 3**
Divide the dough into balls of 270 g each and shape them into balls. Cover the rounds and let them rise for 5 hours at room temperature.
Preheat your oven to its maximum temperature.
Place the rounds on a floured work surface. Punch down with your fingers from the centre outward, flattening them in the middle but leaving nice, airy dough at the edges.
Using your hands, carefully stretch them out to the desired size.
Add toppings of your choice.
Bake the pizzas briefly until done.

# TRADITIONAL FRENCH BAGUETTE

The baguette: perhaps France's most iconic bread. Long, crispy, and with an aroma that once you smell it, you never forget. But though virtually synonymous with France today, the baguette is a fairly young recipe, dating back only to 1920–specifically, to a change in French law that prohibited French bakers from working night shifts. So, to ensure that they could get warm bread onto Parisian breakfast tables, they needed a new, faster recipe they could start in the early morning hours. And so the baguette was born. This version is not particularly fast, but you will taste the extra time in every bite.

**DAY 1**
**Ingredients for preparing the sourdough**
40 g sourdough starter
80 g wheat flour
80 g rye flour
160 g water

**DAY 2**
**Ingredients for the mixing bowl**
1000 g wheat flour
610 g water
20 g salt
6 g baker's yeast
360 g risen sourdough from day 1

## PROCEDURE

**DAY 1**
Combine all the ingredients for the sourdough and let rise for 12 hours at room temperature.

**DAY 2**
In the bowl of a mixer, knead the flour and water together at low speed for 3 minutes. Let stand for 1 hour.
Add the sourdough, yeast and salt. Knead for 8 minutes at low speed and 1 minute at high speed or until the dough temperature reaches 23 °C. Cover the dough with cling film to prevent it from drying out. Let rest for 40 minutes in the bowl.
Stretch and fold your dough once. Set aside in the fridge for 12 hours.

**DAY 3**
Divide the dough into sections of 300 g and shape them into rounds. Let rest for 10 minutes.
Using your hands, roll each baguette to the desired length. Place them on a floured kitchen towel and let them rise for one and a half hours until they have doubled in volume.
Carefully transfer each loaf to a baking sheet. Score each baguette with three diagonal cuts. Bake at 250 °C for 20 minutes. Ensure that there is sufficient steam in the oven during baking.

# BAGUETTE WITH HAM AND CHEESE

This variation on the classic baguette was traditionally made for farmers to take with them into the fields and help get them through their day. The possibilities here are truly endless; try it with different cheeses and discover your own favourite.

**DAY 1**
**Ingredients for preparing the sourdough**
40 g sourdough starter
80 g wheat flour
80 g rye flour
160 g water

**DAY 2**
**Ingredients for the mixing bowl**
1000 g wheat flour
610 g water
20 g salt
6 g baker's yeast
360 g risen sourdough from day 1

**DAY 2**
**Filling**
grated cheese; ham, cubed or thinly sliced

## PROCEDURE

**DAY 1**
Combine all the ingredients for the sourdough and let rise for 12 hours at room temperature.

**DAY 2**
In the bowl of a mixer, knead the flour and water at low speed for 3 minutes. Let it stand for 1 hour.
Add the sourdough, yeast and salt and knead for 8 minutes at low speed and 1 minute at high speed, or until the dough temperature reaches 23 °C. Cover the dough with cling film to prevent it from drying out. Let it rest for 40 minutes in the bowl. Stretch and fold your dough once. Set aside in the fridge for 12 hours.

**DAY 3**
Divide the dough into sections of 300 g per baguette. Stretch the dough and fill each with the grated cheese and ham. Close them by pulling the back of the dough up over the filling. Carefully seal them with your fingers.
Using your hands, roll each baguette to the desired length. Place them on a floured kitchen towel and let rise for one and a half hours until they have doubled in volume.
Carefully transfer each loaf to a baking sheet. Score each baguette with three diagonal cuts. Bake at 250 °C for 20 minutes. Ensure that there is sufficient steam in the oven during baking.

# FOCACCIA

Focaccia is an Italian bread, and one of the oldest kinds of bread that is still being made every day. Originally it was baked on hot stones or in wood-fired ovens, often with no more than olive oil and sea salt. It is still a beloved breakfast bread or daytime snack in the villages along the Ligurian coast. Its impossibly airy crumb, crunchy crust and olive oil aroma have made this bread a favorite in modern cuisine, and it almost always makes the centrepiece of a meal.

**DAY 1**
**Ingredients for preparing the sourdough**
40 g sourdough starter
80 g wheat flour
80 g water

**DAY 2**
**Ingredients for the mixing bowl**
750 g wheat flour
600 g water
40 g potato starch
75 g water
75 g olive oil
15 g salt
200 g risen sourdough from day 1

**Topping**
cherry tomatoes, olive oil, rosemary, sea salt, olives, pepper, cheese

## PROCEDURE

**DAY 1**
Combine all the ingredients for the sourdough and let rise for 12 hours at room temperature.

**DAY 2**
Knead the potato starch with the water. Let stand for 10 minutes.
In the bowl of a mixer, combine all other ingredients with the potato starch mixture.
Knead for 5 minutes at low speed and 5 minutes at high speed or until the dough temperature reaches 23 °C. Cover the dough with cling film to prevent it from drying out. Let the dough rest for 10 minutes in the mixing bowl.
Stretch and fold your dough three times, each 30 minutes apart.
Set the dough aside in the fridge overnight.

**DAY 3**
Remove the dough from the fridge and spread it out on an oiled baking sheet. Every 20 minutes, stretch the dough out a little until it covers the entire baking sheet.
With your fingers, make impressions in the dough. Top with your selected toppings.
Bake the focaccia at 250 °C for 25 minutes.
Ensure that there is sufficient steam in the oven during baking.

## VISITING WITH...

# KÄDI HELSTEIN

During a bread delivery to a new hotel, I met Kädi Helstein, an Estonian chef who, like me, is obsessed with sourdough. We clicked right away and she opened up about her life. The unique bread that she makes with sourdough, quite frankly, blew my mind. It's funny how sometimes you can come across someone who can completely expand your vision of bread. And that's exactly what happened with Kädi, who came to Norway to gain experience in the trade.

Even the very first time we met I could tell that this was someone who had an exceptional passion for cooking, fermentation and tradition. Kädi told me about her life in Estonia and the restaurant she had grown up in: Hämsa Maheresto, in Võrumaa, a country town in the south of Estonia. It's a place where tradition and the modern craft come together, and where her family has been serving local, natural and honest food for decades.

Southern Estonia and Northern Estonia are very different in terms of landscape, culture, and atmosphere. The north is coastal, very flat, and quite developed, with Tallinn, a modern international capital, as its centre of gravity. Here you will hear primarily standard Estonian and you will feel the influence of Western Europe. The South is hilly, forested and much quieter, dotted with villages where tradition and nature reign. In regions like Võru and Setomaa, where Kädi comes from, the people still speak in dialect and folk culture lives on. Where the north feels faster and more modern, the south offers a deeper and more comfortable connection with the land and its customs.

From an early age, Kädi was closely engaged with both the kitchen and the traditional dishes that her family served, like locally smoked meats and foraged ingredients. Obsessed with baking, she introduced the sourdough breads to the restaurant. Today she's known as a driven and creative chef. According to a TV news report, the restaurant has been crowned with the title of best regional dish, and her mother specifically was

lauded for her competence as hostess and chef. Kädi's devotion to quality and the guest experience is absolutely clear, both in and out of the kitchen. Today her two children, Eliise and Hannes, also help out with the family business.

The restaurant is known not only for its charming atmosphere and fresh ingredients, but also for the particular bread that they bake daily: must leib, the traditional Estonian black bread. Dark, aromatic and with character. Bread that stays with you. Often made with rye, in combination with linseed or other seeds.

Also notable: in 2023 the restaurant was crowned the first organic restaurant in Võrumaa. If you ever happen to travel to Estonia, I couldn't give you a better tip: Hämsa Maheresto, surrounded by nature, just outside Võru, a restaurant offering you the authentic experience of South Estonian cuisine. Traditional ways and hospitality that touches you. You never eat there alone–you're part of a story. With local and organic food as the main characters.

What struck me most about Kädi's sourdough bread was the balance between technique and feel. She works with organic rye and other local grains. Her sourdough starter has been alive for years, nurtured with rhythm and care. She explained to me how bread from Hämsa knows no haste. She has spent years perfecting the recipe. Her bread knows rest and patience, just like mine. Everything in her baking process is attuned to attention, timing and trust.

Even though I met Kädi far from her home, the bread that we baked together clearly carried her Estonian roots.

My meeting with Kädi reminded me of how universal sourdough is, and at the same time how personal. Her bread carries the scent of the Estonian countryside, the wisdom of generations, and the hand of a woman who knows her trade but forges her own path within it. It was an unexpected meeting, but one that will stay in my memory for a long time.

# KÄDI'S MUST LEIB

The recipe for this hearty sourdough bread comes from a friend from Estonia, where rye is an important element of the culinary culture. This traditional bread is unique to Estonia; its name means simply "black" (*must*) "bread" (*leib*). It owes its dark colour to the fact that the recipe uses only rye.

**DAY 1**
**Ingredients for preparing the sourdough**
50 g sourdough starter
250 g rye flour
250 g water

**DAY 2**
**Ingredients for the mixing bowl**
100 g ground rye malt
500 g wholemeal rye flour
125 g brown sugar
390 g water
40 g salt
550 g risen sourdough from day 1

## PROCEDURE

**DAY 1**

Combine all the ingredients for the sourdough and let rise for 12 hours at room temperature.

**DAY 2**

Place all ingredients in a mixing bowl. Mix by hand until all the flour is incorporated.
Divide the dough into three parts of 800 g each and transfer to a greased baking tin.
Let it rise in a warm place for 3 hours.
Bake each bread at 220 °C for 15 minutes, lower the heat to 180 °C, and bake for a further 40 minutes.

# CIABATTA

*Ciabatta* is literally the Italian word for "slipper," but it also means the flat, wide shape of this popular bread. It is a modern bread, developed in Northern Italy in the 1980s as an answer to France's baguette–but it became an instant classic in its own right. What makes ciabatta so extraordinary is the extremely wet dough and high hydration. This is what gives it its characteristic open crumb and flaky, golden-brown crust. But it also means this dough requires a gentle touch, lots of rest, and minimum handling to preserve that airiness.

**DAY 1**
**Ingredients for preparing the sourdough**
10 g sourdough starter
20 g wheat flour
20 g rye flour
40 g water

**DAY 2**
**Ingredients for the autolysis**
400 g wheat flour
320 g water

**DAY 2**
**Ingredients to add after the autolysis**
8 g salt
10 g olive oil
90 g risen sourdough from day 1

## PROCEDURE

**DAY 1**

Combine all the ingredients for the sourdough and let rise for 12 hours at room temperature.

**DAY 2**

Put all the ingredients for the autolysis in the bowl of a mixer. Knead for 4 minutes at low speed. Cover the dough with cling film to prevent it from drying out. Perform an autolysis of 30 minutes. Add the salt, sourdough and olive oil and knead for 8 minutes at high speed.
Let the dough rest for 10 minutes in the mixing bowl.
Stretch and fold your dough three times, each 30 minutes apart.
Set aside in the fridge overnight.

**DAY 3**

Remove the dough from the fridge to a floured work surface and divide it into 6 equal parts.
Carefully transfer them to a baking sheet with the cut side up.
Let rise 2 hours at room temperature.
Bake the ciabattas at 240 °C for 8 minutes.
Ensure that there is sufficient steam in the oven during baking.

# SPANISH TAPAS BREAD

In Spain, life revolves around coming together at the dining table, and bread is always there. Tapas bread is often a small crispy slice of the perfect bread to stack with olives, tomatoes or ham: it has a firm crust and a spongy interior that is equally good at soaking up creamy spreads as it is oils and sauces. In some regions it is lightly toasted or rubbed with garlic and tomato. It's a bread that invites sharing, just like tapas.

**DAY 1**
**Ingredients for preparing the sourdough**
20 g sourdough starter
40 g wheat flour
40 g water

**DAY 2**
**Ingredients for the autolysis**
400 g wheat flour
100 g wheat meal
360 g water

**DAY 2**
**Ingredients to add after the autolysis**
12 g salt
100 g risen sourdough from day 1

**Additions**
120 g coarsely chopped olives
80 g sun-dried tomatoes
4 g dried thyme
1 tablespoon olive oil

## PROCEDURE

**DAY 1**

Combine all the ingredients for the sourdough and let rise for 12 hours at room temperature.

**DAY 2**

Put all the ingredients for the autolysis in the mixing bowl. Knead for 4 minutes at low speed. Cover the dough with cling film to prevent it from drying out. Perform an autolysis of 20 minutes. Add the salt and sourdough, and then knead for 3 minutes at medium speed.
Switch to low speed and knead the olives, tomatoes, thyme and olive oil into the dough for 1 minute until they are fully incorporated.
Let the dough rest for 10 minutes in the mixing bowl.
Stretch and fold your dough three times, each 30 minutes apart.
Let the bread rise for approximately five hours, until it has nearly doubled in volume.
Shape the dough into a long loaf and transfer to a floured proofing basket covered with a kitchen towel. Let it rest overnight in the fridge.

**DAY 3**

Place the dough on a baking sheet. Score it several times to give the finished bread an artisan look. Bake for 15 minutes at 235 °C; then reduce heat to 220 °C and bake for a further 30 minutes. Ensure that there is sufficient steam in the oven during baking.

# TURKISH SIMIT

Simit is a much-loved street bread in Turkey, but its distinctive circle shape and crispy, sesame seed-coated crust is well known in other countries as well. Before it goes into the oven, the dough goes quickly into boiling water with molasses to give it that shiny and crunchy exterior. Simit is often eaten at breakfast, with tea and cheese, or as a quick snack for on the road. A bread full of character, simplicity and tradition, straight from the streets of Istanbul.

**DAY 1**
**Ingredients for preparing the sourdough**
30 g sourdough starter
60 g wheat flour
60 g water

**DAY 2**
**Ingredients for the mixing bowl**
490 g wheat flour
285 g water
20 g molasses
10 g salt
150 g risen sourdough from day 1

**Coating**
40 g molasses
125 g boiling water
200 g sesame seeds

## PROCEDURE

**DAY 1**

Combine all the ingredients for the sourdough and let rise for 12 hours at room temperature.

**DAY 2**

Place all ingredients in the bowl of a mixer. Knead for 3 minutes at low speed and 8 minutes at high speed. Cover the dough with cling film to prevent it from drying out.
Let rest in the bowl for 30 minutes.
Stretch and fold your dough once.
Let the dough rise for approximately 4 hours until it has nearly doubled in volume. Divide the dough into 6 pieces of 160 g each. Roll each piece out and connect the ends of each piece of dough to make a circle. Let rise for 2 hours.
For the coating, pour the boiling water over the molasses and stir until all the molasses is absorbed.
Dunk the risen dough carefully in the molasses water for a few seconds, and then dip in the sesame seeds. Transfer to a baking sheet and bake at 210 °C for 25 minutes.
Ensure that there is sufficient steam in the oven during baking.

# GUINNESS BREAD

This bread gets its dark colour from the addition of Guinness, the iconic Irish stout. The warming bitterness of the beer complements the rich, acidic aromas of the sourdough to create a surprisingly full and unique bread. Together, sourdough and Guinness make a firm bread with soft crumb and crunchy crust, perfect to accompany winter dishes. A wink and a nod to Irish traditions, baked in a contemporary style.

**DAY 1**

**Ingredients for preparing the sourdough**

20 g sourdough starter
40 g wheat flour
40 g water

**DAY 2**

**Ingredients for the autolysis**

300 g wheat flour
200 g wheat meal
370 g Guinness
10 g dark malt powder (optional)
10 g salt
100 g risen sourdough from day 1

## PROCEDURE

**DAY 1**

Combine all the ingredients for the sourdough and let rise for 12 hours at room temperature.

**DAY 2**

Put all the ingredients for the autolysis in the mixing bowl.
Knead for 4 minutes at low speed and 6 minutes at high speed.
Cover the dough with cling film to prevent it from drying out.
Perform an autolysis of 40 minutes.
Stretch and fold your dough three times, each 30 minutes apart.
Let the bread rise for approximately five hours, until it has nearly doubled in volume.
Shape the dough and place it in a floured proofing basket covered with a kitchen towel. Set aside in the fridge for 8 to 36 hours. The longer it stays in the fridge, the more flavor it will have.

**DAY 3**

Place the dough on a baking sheet and score it. Bake for 15 minutes at 235 °C; then reduce heat to 220 °C and bake for a further 30 minutes.
Ensure that there is sufficient steam in the oven during baking.

# CORSICAN FRUIT BREAD

This traditional Corsican bread is a feast for the taste buds, full of sweet raisins and crunchy walnuts. The bread has a soft, slightly sweet crumb and a firm texture, perfect with coffee or as a breakfast bread. In Corsica, this bread is often baked during holidays, when it serves as a symbol of abundance and pleasure. An inviting and artisinal bread that captures the rich flavors of the island in each bite.

**DAY 1**
**Ingredients for preparing the sourdough**
20 g sourdough starter
40 g wheat flour
40 g water

**DAY 2**
**Ingredients for soaking**
120 g raisins
130 g water
100 g brandy

**DAY 2**
**Ingredients for the autolysis**
500 g t80 wheat flour
330 g water

**DAY 2**
**Ingredients to add after the autolysis**
75 g butter
125 g sugar
10 g salt
100 g risen sourdough from day 1
120 g coarsely chopped walnuts
soaked raisins

## PROCEDURE

**DAY 1**
Combine all the ingredients for the sourdough and let rise for 12 hours at room temperature.

**DAY 2**
Soak the raisins in the brandy and water.
Put the ingredients for the autolysis in the mixing bowl.
Knead for 4 minutes at low speed. Cover the dough with cling film to prevent it from drying out. Perform an autolysis of 20 minutes.
Add the butter, sugar, salt and sourdough and knead for 8 minutes at high speed. Adjust the speed to low, add the walnuts and soaked raisins, and knead for another 2 minutes until they are fully incorporated.
Let the dough rest for 10 minutes in the mixing bowl.
Stretch and fold your dough three times, each 30 minutes apart.
Let the dough rise for approximately 5 hours until it has nearly doubled in volume.
Shape the dough and place it in a floured proofing basket covered with a kitchen towel. Let it rest overnight in the fridge.

**DAY 3**
Place the dough on a baking sheet and score it. Bake for 15 minutes at 235 °C; then reduce heat to 220 °C and bake for a further 30 minutes.
Ensure that there is sufficient steam in the oven during baking.

# TORTILLA

The original corn tortilla was made in Mexico thousands of years before the arrival of the Spanish and was an important part of Mexican food culture. The Spanish introduced wheat flour to Northern Mexico, leading to the development of flour tortillas. The word "tortilla" itself is Spanish and derives from the Spanish word "torta," meaning "cake," which was used to describe the flatbread.

**DAY 1**
**Ingredients for preparing the sourdough**
40 g sourdough starter
80 g wheat flour
80 g water

**DAY 2**
**Ingredients for the mixing bowl**
420 g wheat flour
160 g water
11 g salt
60 g olive oil
200 g risen sourdough from day 1

## PROCEDURE

**DAY 1**
Combine all the ingredients for the sourdough and let rise for 12 hours at room temperature.

**DAY 2**
Place all ingredients in the bowl of a mixer.
Knead for 4 minutes at low speed and 2 minutes at high speed.
Cover the dough with cling film to prevent it from drying out.
Let rise at room temperature for 12 to 18 hours.

**DAY 3**
Divide the dough into 12 pieces of 70 g each. Place them on a floured work surface and roll them out into circles 0.3 cm thick.
In a preheated pan, fry the tortillas for approximately 3 minutes on each side.

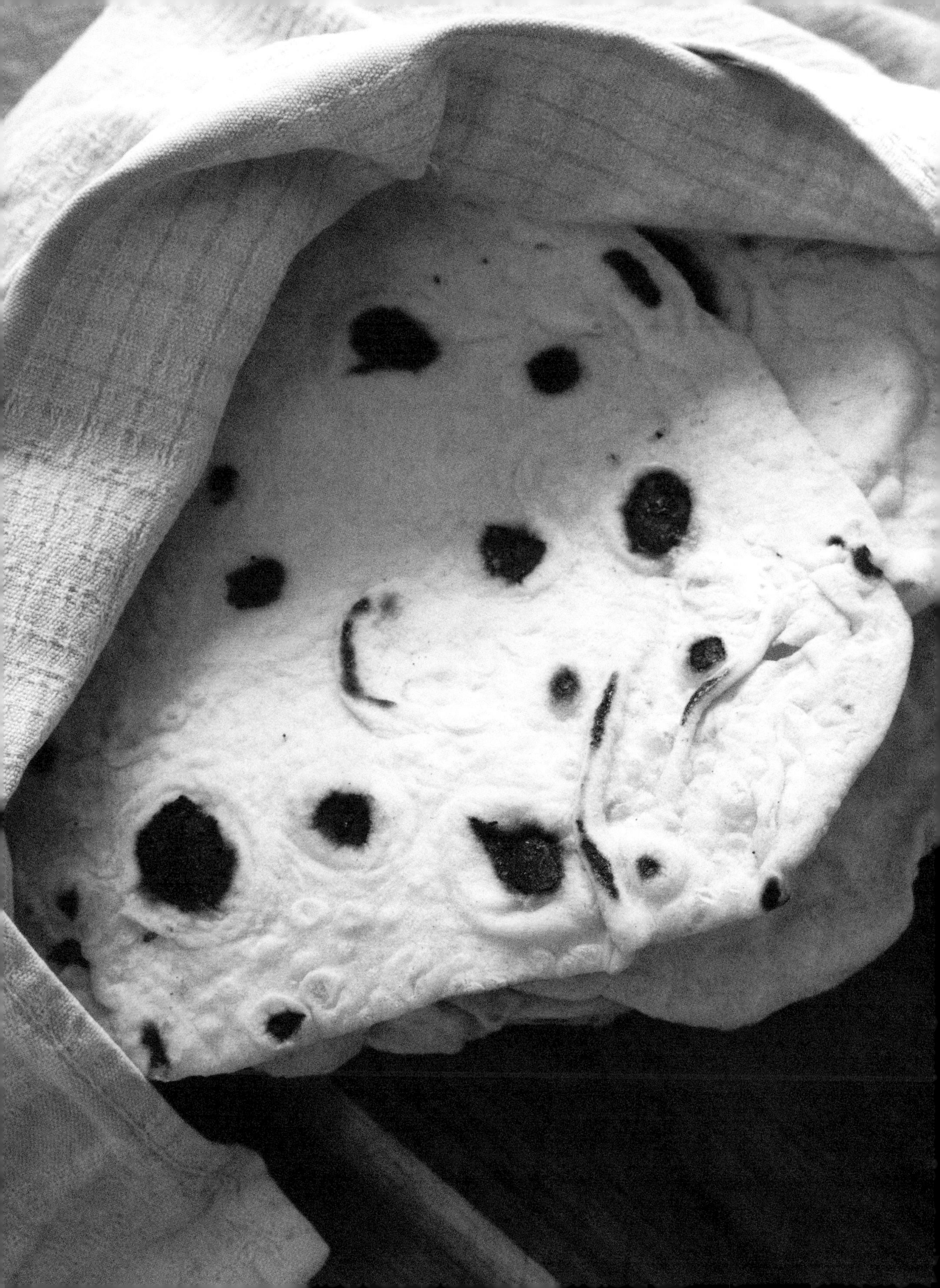

# SWEDISH KNÄCKEBRÖD

Knäckebröd is a traditional crispy bread from Sweden; it's usually made from rye, and it has a clean, slightly sour taste. It's been made in the Nordic countries for centuries because it stays fresh for a very long time, just the thing for the long Scandinavian winters. This thin, crispy bread has a firm bite and holds its own against many different toppings, from butter and cheese to herring and salmon. Simple, nutritious and an indispensable attribute of the Swedish dining table.

**DAY 1**
**Ingredients for preparing the sourdough**
20 g sourdough starter
40 g rye flour
40 g water

**DAY 2**
**Ingredients for the mixing bowl**
280 g wheat meal
100 g rye flour
280 g water
8 g salt
120 g seeds of your choice
100 g risen sourdough from day 1

## PROCEDURE

**DAY 1**
Combine all the ingredients for the sourdough and let rise for 12 hours at room temperature.

**DAY 2**
Put all ingredients in a mixing bowl and knead by hand until all the flour has been incorporated, about 4 minutes. Cover the dough with cling film to prevent it from drying out.
Let rise for 4 hours at room temperature and then set aside in the fridge overnight.

**DAY 3**
Divide the dough into 17 pieces of 45 g each. On a well-floured work surface, roll the dough out in the desired shape as thinly as possible—around 0.2 cm. Carefully transfer to a baking sheet. Bake at 180 °C for 9 minutes.

# VISITING WITH THE PURATOS SOURDOUGH LIBRARY IN SANKT VITH
# KARL DE SMEDT

Nestled among the wild, rolling hills of eastern Belgium, tucked away in tiny Sankt Vith, you will find a place that at first sight might look like a modern research centre. But open the doors of the Sourdough Institute and you will walk into a world where time, flavor and culture are preserved with a devotion bordering on the religious. This is the Puratos Sourdough Library, the only sourdough library in the world.

It is a library not of books, but a catalogue of living cultures: over 150 different sourdough starters from all corners of the earth, quietly resting in temperature-regulated chambers. Meticulously numbered, nurtured and analyzed. Each of these starters carries the unique microflora of its own region, its baker, its tradition–from an Italian starter that has been handed down within the same family for centuries to a Japanese sourdough that is fed on rice.

It was here that I met Karl De Smedt, the "librarian" of this living archive, with all the bearing and passion of a man who sees sourdough not only as science but as cultural heritage. As we walked down the gleaming corridors, he told me tales of sourdough as cultural DNA: how starters from the same family can still taste very different, how you can trace the migration patterns of bakers through the microbiomes of their sourdough. The yeasts in the sourdough sometimes come from the flour, but they also have to do with who has fed them. Or the altitude of the bakery.

Thanks to this library, we now know things that would have never come to light without it. There are cases where Karl has found a specific dominating yeast when women have fed the sourdough rather than men. Or there is the specific yeast that Karl found in three sourdoughs from bakeries on three different continents, sharing nothing in common except one thing: they are all at an altitude of 1500 metres.

The sourdough library was established primarily to preserve the biodiversity of the sourdoughs. When the library receives a new sourdough, they set aside a small sample that is sent to a university in Bolzano, Italy, where it is thinned out and placed in a fermentation chamber. A few days later, they then analyze the newly formed strains. The DNA is then tested and identified. At this point, the library has isolated more than

1400 different strains of bacteria and yeast in the various sourdoughs. They are all stored in the library at a temperature of -80 °C.

Every starter in the library is different. They come from Italy, France, Japan, Mexico, Lebanon, Peru, Brazil, and many other places. Some are generations old and have been handed down from great-great-grandmothers to their great-great-grandchildren. Others come from monasteries or remote islands. Each jar contains a living community of yeasts and lactic acids the composition of which depends on the type of flour, the climate, the hands that have tended them, and in some cases even the wood from the spoon used to stir them.

This library houses something very special: a community united by fermentation. Every jar in the refrigerated chamber tells a story, a secret recipe, a family history, a region. The library is a repository not only for the product, but also for the soul of bread-baking: different everywhere, but alive everywhere.

What if a baker dies without someone to continue their starter? Or if someone accidentally uses up all of a starter? Or all the sourdoughs that have been burned to ash in bakery fires? For these and others, there is Puratos Sourdough Library, securing the future of sourdough baking.

What struck me about the Sourdough Library is not only the scientific precision, but the understanding that we as bakers, chefs, home breadmakers and fans of good bread all make up part of a larger chain. Every time that we feed our starter, every time that we slice bread, we are continuing something that has been growing for centuries.

# INJERA

Injera is the traditional sourdough bread from Ethipoia and Eritrea, made from teff flour. Teff is a traditional grain from the Horn of Africa, where it has been cultivated for at least four thousand years and still grows excellently in the highlands of Ethiopia, where it is an important staple in the Ethiopian diet. It is a small, nutritious grain, rich in iron and proteins. And it is one of the oldest cultivated grains in the world. In injera it is fermented for a long time, which gives the bread its distinct sour flavor and spongy texture.

**DAY 1**
**Ingredients for preparing the sourdough**
50 g sourdough starter
500 g teff flour
500 g water

**DAY 2**
**Ingredients for the mixing bowl**
280 g wheat meal
500 g water
8 g baker's yeast
1050 g risen sourdough from day 1

## PROCEDURE

**DAY 1**
Combine all the ingredients for the sourdough and let rise for 12 hours at room temperature.

**DAY 2**
Put all the ingredients in a mixing bowl and mix with a hand mixer until everything is incorporated, about 5 minutes.
Let the batter rise for 3 hours at room temperature.
For each bread, fry 150 g of the batter in a preheated hot pan on the stove.

# FOUGASSE

Fougasse is the French version of Italian focaccia. Shaped to look like an olive branch, it brings something fun and aesthetic to the kitchen table. This light and airy bread was once used to test the temperature of a wood-fired oven.

**DAY 1**
**Ingredients for preparing the sourdough**
50 g sourdough starter
100 g wheat flour
100 g water

**DAY 2**
**Ingredients for the mixing bowl**
1000 g wheat flour
600 g water
22 g salt
4 g baker's yeast
250 g risen sourdough from day 1

**DAY 2**
**Ingredients for the bassinage**
50 g water
70 g olive oil

**Topping**
200 g olive oil
1 stalk of basil
3 cloves garlic

## PROCEDURE

**DAY 1**
Combine all the ingredients for the sourdough and let rise for 12 hours at room temperature.

**DAY 2**
Place all ingredients in the bowl of a mixer. Knead for 4 minutes at low speed and 6 minutes at high speed. Add the water for the bassinage. Cover with cling film to keep it from drying out. Stretch and fold the bassinage into your dough. Stretch and fold the dough again after 30 minutes and then again 30 minutes later.
Let your dough rise for 2 hours at room temperature and then set aside in the fridge overnight.

**DAY 3**
Remove the dough from the fridge and divide into 4 parts of 500 g each. Round them and let rest for 20 minutes. Shape the dough into a leaf and let rise for 2 hours.
Use your dough cutter to cut the lines of the "veins" of the olive leaf: 3 lines left, 3 lines right and 1 line at the top. Spread these carefully with your fingers.
Combine the olive oil, the peeled garlic and the basil, and spread over each leaf.
Bake at 260 °C for 12 minutes.

# LYON CROWN

This wheat bread has been made for generations in the French city of Lyon. It is not scored, so the bread decides where the steam is going to escape. This gives it a very rustic and artisan look, and makes every loaf unique.

**DAY 1**
**Ingredients for preparing the sourdough**
20 g sourdough starter
60 g wheat flour
60 g water

**DAY 2**
**Ingredients for the autolysis**
800 g wheat flour
190 g wheat meal
640 g water
140 g fermented bread dough (optional)

**DAY 2**
**Ingredients to add after the autolysis**
22 g salt
140 g risen sourdough from day 1

## PROCEDURE

**DAY 1**
Combine all the ingredients for the sourdough and let rise for 12 hours at room temperature.

**DAY 2**
Put all the ingredients for the autolysis in the bowl of a mixer. Knead for 6 minutes at low speed. Perform an autolysis of 20 minutes.
Knead the sourdough and the salt through the dough for 8 minutes or until it reaches a dough temperature of 23 °C. Cover the dough with cling film to prevent it from drying out. Let the dough rest for 10 minutes in the mixing bowl.
Stretch and fold your dough three times, each 30 minutes apart. Let the bread rise for approximately 5 hours, until it has nearly doubled in volume.
Make a hole in the middle with your thumb, so you get a circle. Place it in a round floured proofing basket (in Lyon they have a specific basket for this bread). Let it rest overnight in the fridge.

**DAY 3**
Place the dough on a baking sheet. For the best-looking end result, do not score. Bake the bread at 250 °C for 15 minutes; then lower the temperature to 225 °C and bake for a further 30 minutes.
Ensure that there is sufficient steam in the oven during baking.

# IRISH BIRLEY

An Irish classic, made from a combination of wheat, spelt and barley. Barley is one of the more difficult flours to work with; it contains little gluten, so barley breads are generally more compact.

**DAY 1**
**Ingredients for preparing the sourdough**
20 g sourdough starter
40 g wheat flour
40 g water

**DAY 2**
**Ingredients for the mixing bowl**
200 g wheat flour
200 g spelt flour
100 g barley
13 g salt
100 g risen sourdough from day 1

## PROCEDURE

**DAY 1**

Combine all the ingredients for the sourdough and let rise for 12 hours at room temperature.

**DAY 2**

Place all ingredients in the bowl of a mixer. Knead for 4 minutes at low speed and 6 minutes at high speed. Cover the dough with cling film to prevent it from drying out.
Stretch and fold your dough three times, each 30 minutes apart.
Let the dough rise for 4 hours at room temperature.
Shape the bread and place it in a floured proofing basket covered with a kitchen towel. Let it rest overnight in the fridge.

**DAY 3**

Place the dough on a baking sheet and score it in a traditional manner. Bake for 15 minutes at 235 °C; then reduce heat to 220 °C and bake for a further 30 minutes.
Ensure that there is sufficient steam in the oven during baking.

V

# DELUXE BREADS

# BREAD WITH FRUIT À LA COUPE

This rich fruit bread is filled with a luxurious mix of dried dates, prunes and apricots, which give it a deep, natural sweetness and a soft texture.

**DAY 1**
**Ingredients for preparing the sourdough**
20 g sourdough starter
40 g wheat flour
40 g rye flour
80 g water

**DAY 2**
**Ingredients for the mixing bowl**
700 g t65 wheat flour
200 g t150 wheat meal
100 g buckwheat
700 g water
22 g salt
180 g risen sourdough from day 1

**Fruit**
100 g dates, chopped
100 g apricots, chopped
200 g prunes, chopped

## PROCEDURE

**DAY 1**
Combine all the ingredients for the sourdough and let rise for 12 hours at room temperature.

**DAY 2**
Place all ingredients in the bowl of a mixer.
Knead for 3 minutes at low speed and 4 minutes at high speed or until the dough reaches a temperature of 23 °C. Cover the dough with cling film to prevent it from drying out.
Knead the fruit into the dough for 1 minute at low speed.
Let the dough rest for 10 minutes in the mixing bowl.
Stretch and fold your dough three times, each 30 minutes apart.
Let the bread rise for approximately 5 hours, until it has nearly doubled in volume.
Shape the dough and place it in a floured proofing basket covered with a kitchen towel. Set aside in the fridge overnight.

**DAY 3**
Place the dough on a baking sheet and score it in a traditional manner. Bake at 250 °C for 45 minutes.

# DELUXE RYE BREAD WITH FRUIT

This rye bread is a rich variation on the traditional rye bread, enriched with a mix of dried fruits like raisins, figs and prunes. The sourdough gives the bread a deep, slightly sour edge that perfectly complements the sweetness of the fruit. Because of its tight, firm structure it is ideal as a hearty breakfast or filling lunch. It puts a surprising twist on the rye bread you know.

**DAY 1**
**Ingredients for preparing the sourdough**
80 g sourdough starter
160 g rye flour
160 g water

**DAY 2**
**Ingredients for the mixing bowl**
250 g t170 whole-meal rye flour
250 g t85 rye flour
400 g 60 °C water
12 g salt
400 g risen sourdough from day 1

**Fruit**
100 g raisins
100 g figs, chopped
100 g prunes, chopped

## PROCEDURE

**DAY 1**
Combine all the ingredients for the sourdough and let rise for 12 hours at room temperature.

**DAY 2**
Place all ingredients in the bowl of a mixer. Using the K beater attachment, mix for 6 minutes at low speed and 1 minute at high speed, or until the dough reaches a temperature of 35 °C.
Switch the speed to low and mix the fruit into the dough for 1 minute.
With wet hands, divide the dough into two pieces of 800 g each.
Place them in greased baking tins. Cover the dough with cling film to prevent it from drying out.
Let rise for 5 hours.
Bake the two loaves at 250 °C for 40 minutes.

## VISITING WITH...

# BOUDEWIJN NIJMEIJER

When I arrived at House of Bakers, Boudewijn Nijmeijer's bakery and patisserie, the passion in the air was palpable. It's not without reason that Boudewijn is known as the undisputed master of panettone in all the Benelux and beyond. His reputation precedes him, but more than anything else it's his dedication to his craft that impresses. And he's been making an impression in the patisserie world since a very early age.

I met Boudewijn Nijmeijer through Michel Ernots, cofounder of The Pastry Academy, where I studied in Las Vegas. Michel told me that Boudewijn sends him a panettone, all the way from the Netherlands to the USA, every Christmas.

"I always want to be the best," Boudewijn told me. And I could see how that drive for perfection took him to the top of the patisserie world.

In 2012 he won the "Golden Whisk", a leading competition for talented pastry chefs, which he followed up by winning the Dutch Pastry Awards in 2014. In 2015 his chocolate bonbon was proclaimed the best in the Netherlands.

In his bright, modern workspace I saw row after well-organized row of containers: flour, raisins, sugar, citrus zest... everything needed to make the perfect panettone, that iconic Italian Christmas bread so sought after around the world, and so airy, tasty and complex when done right. Boudewijn explained to me that panettone is more than just a matter of kneading dough–it's a delicate process in which fermentation, hydration and timing are everything.

"Panettone is a good story in itself," Boudewijn told me as he deftly folded the dough. "You have to give it attention, all the time it needs to grow and develop its character."

What still sticks with me most is his dedication to perfection and tradition, but also his openness to innovation. He combines Italian techniques with a modern perspective on the science of dough, which together give his breads their unmistakable style: light as air, yet rich in aroma.

As we worked, Boudewijn told me about his long career, from his work in patisseries in the Middle East to his many prizes. But he seemed proudest about representing the Netherlands in the panettone world championships in Milan, an experience that dramatically

expanded both his vision and his professional skills. House of Bakers is more than just a business to him; it's a place where tradition and modern professionalism come together, where every bread is made with respect and passion. And anyone who visits here can taste that immediately in every product.

After hours of patience and precision, our panettone comes out of the oven, perfectly baked, golden brown, with a smell that you can't resist and a crumb that's soft and springy. It is a moment of pride and admiration.

My visit to Boudewijn Nijmeijer and House of Bakers showed me that panettone is much more than a Christmas bread: it's a craft, a story, and most of all an art that you can only make with your heart and soul. The Netherlands can take pride in calling Boudewijn the country's best pastry chef.

# PANETTONE DELUXE BY BOUDEWIJN NIJMEIJER

This is a classic panettone based on pasta madre. The two-stage fermentation gives the crumb an airy texture and a balanced flavor. The panettone contains brandied raisins, confit oranges, honey and vanilla, and is coated in an almond glaze. The process demands precision and patience: the dough must rise multiple times, and after baking, it must be hung upside-down to prevent it from collapsing. In this, Boudewijn follows the traditional method, with attention to detail and ingredients of the highest quality.

**FOR FIVE 1-KG CAKES**

**First dough**
790 g strong flour
400 g water
240 g pasta madre (sourdough starter)
300 g sugar
285 g egg yolks
330 g butter

**Second dough**
310 g flour
125 g water
220 g sugar
240 g egg yolks
480 g butter
70 g honey
50 g orange paste
marrow from 4 vanilla beans
540 g brandied raisins
540 g candied orange pieces
18 g salt

**Finishing touches**
pearl sugar
whole almonds

## PROCEDURE

**DAY 1 ACTIVATING THE PASTA MADRE**

**6.00 AM—First activation**
Activate the pasta madre with a ratio of 1:1:0.45 (starter:flour:water). Let rise in a proofing chamber at 28 °C for approximately 3.5 hours, until a pH of 4.1 is reached.

**9.30 AM—Second activation**
Repeat the same ratios and fermentation at 28 °C for another 3.5 hours, once again up to a pH of 4.1.

**DAY 1 PREPARATION OF THE FIRST DOUGH**

Dissolve the sugar in warm water.
Add the flour and mix at low speed for approximately 20 minutes, until you observe strong gluten formation.
Add the egg yolks gradually, one-third at a time, mixing well after each addition.
Add the butter gradually, one-third at a time, mixing until the dough is fully smooth and elastic.
The temperature of the dough needs to end at around 26 °C.
Then let the dough rise in a proofing chamber at 25 °C for 12 to 16 hours, until it has tripled in volume.

**DAY 2 PREPARATION OF THE SECOND DOUGH**

Add the flour to the first dough and mix at low speed for approximately 20 minutes, until you observe good gluten formation.

Add the sugar, honey, vanilla and orange paste and mix thoroughly.

Add the butter gradually, one-third at a time, while mixing at high speed.

Still mixing at high speed, add the egg yolks gradually, one-third at a time, until you have a supple and strong dough.

Add the water gradually, one-fourth at a time, taking care not to lose the structure of the dough.

Finally, carefully fold the raisins and candied orange pieces into the dough with a spatula.

**DAY 2 SHAPING AND RISING**

Carefully fold the dough and let rest for 60 minutes.

Divide the dough into portions of 1000 g. Shape each portion into a round, keeping tension high, and let rest 30 minutes.

Shape each round into a panettone. and place into the forms.

Proof at 28 °C for 7 to 8 hours, until the dough is just peeking above the edge of the form.

Remove each pannetone from the proofing chamber and let rest for 1 hour at room temperature before baking.

**DAY 2 BAKING**

Apply the almond glaze to the top of each panettone.

Sprinkle with pearl sugar and whole almonds.

Bake at 170 °C until you reach a core temperature of 93 °C, approximately 55 minutes.

Immediately after baking, stick skewers through the bottom of each panettone and leave them hanging upside-down to cool.

# SOURDOUGH WITH FIGS

This sourdough bread, with the rich flavors of dried figs and crunchy walnuts, is a true delicacy. The subtle sweetness of the figs and the earthy, nutty flavor of the walnuts together make an elegant pairing that is highlighted by the deep, complex acidity of the sourdough. The result is a luxurious bread with a refined texture, and a rich taste experience suitable for special occasions (or just spoiling yourself). Serve this bread with a cheese plank, a good glass of wine, or as part of a special breakfast. A bread that simply exudes artisanship and class.

**DAY 1**

**Ingredients for preparing the sourdough**

20 g sourdough starter
40 g rye flour
40 g water

**DAY 2**

**Ingredients for the autolysis**

450 g wheat flour
50 g rye flour
350 g water
12 g salt
100 g risen sourdough from day 1

**Additions**

100 g dried figs, coarsely chopped
110 g walnuts, coarsely chopped

## PROCEDURE

**DAY 1**

Combine all the ingredients for the sourdough and let rise for 12 hours at room temperature.

**DAY 2**

Put all the ingredients for the autolysis in the mixing bowl. Knead for 4 minutes at low speed. Cover the dough with cling film to keep it from drying out. Perform an autolysis of 20 minutes.

Add the salt and sourdough and mix for 3 minutes at high speed. Reduce to low speed and knead the figs and walnuts into the dough until they are fully incorporated, about 1 minute.

Let the dough rest for 10 minutes in the mixing bowl.

Stretch and fold your dough three times, each 30 minutes apart.

Let the bread rise for approximately five hours, until it has nearly doubled in volume.

Shape the dough and place it in a floured proofing basket covered with a kitchen towel. Let it rest overnight in the fridge.

**DAY 3**

Place the dough on a baking sheet. Score the bread and then bake it for 15 minutes at 235 °C; reduce heat to 220 °C and bake for a further 30 minutes.

Ensure that there is sufficient steam in the oven during baking.

# KRAMIEK

Kramiek, affectionately referred to as "kramiekje" at home in Flanders, is still beloved in Belgium today but can be traced back to the Middle Ages, when it was made for holidays and special occasions. It is a bread that symbolises abundance, and it was often used as a gift or an element of a religious celebration. Modern Belgians enjoy it, too, albeit with an everyday coffee or breakfast, but it is still a flavorful reminder of the medieval Flemish baking tradition.

**DAY 1**
**Ingredients for preparing the sourdough**
20 g sourdough starter
40 g wheat flour
40 g water

**DAY 2**
**Ingredients for the mixing bowl**
200 g t55 Americana flour
120 g eggs
20 g powdered sugar
5 g salt
4 g baker's yeast
100 g risen sourdough from day 1

**Additions**
80 g butter
130 g dry raisins
80 g powdered sugar

**For soaking the raisins**
130 g raisins
40 g water

**To brush**
1 egg

## PROCEDURE

**DAY 1**
Combine all the ingredients for the sourdough and let rise for 12 hours at room temperature.

**DAY 2**
Hydrate the raisins in the water.
Place all ingredients in the bowl of a mixer. Knead for 5 minutes at low speed and 5 minutes at high speed. Adjust speed to low, add the butter, and knead until you have a smooth dough.
Add the hydrated raisins and the pearl sugar and knead at low speed until everything is incorporated, about 1 minute. Cover with cling film to keep the dough from drying out.
Let the dough rest for 10 minutes in the mixing bowl.
Stretch and fold your dough once. Let rise for approximately 3 hours, until the dough is nearly doubled in volume.
Divide the dough into two parts and shape them. Place each in a greased baking tin. Let rise for two and a half hours. Brush with the egg and score a cross over the top of the dough.
Decorate with pearl sugar and bake at 150 °C for 25 minutes. Ensure that there is sufficient steam in the oven during baking.

# CHOCOLATAELLA

Chocolataella is my own luxurious creation, born from a love of sourdough and a weakness for chocolate. It combines the depth of a well-fermented sourdough bread with the full flavor of cocoa, a pinch of sugar and generously sized chunks of dark chocolate. The result is an intense bread, bordering on a dessert, but still just enough of a bread to work for breakfast or to accompany your morning cup of coffee.

**DAY 1**
**Ingredients for preparing the sourdough**
20 g sourdough starter
40 g wheat flour
40 g water

**DAY 2**
**Ingredients for the autolysis**
500 g wheat flour
360 g water
30 g cocoa powder
50 g sugar (white or brown)
10 g dark malt powder (optional)

**DAY 2**
**Ingredients to add after the autolysis**
150 g chocolate
10 g salt
100 g risen sourdough from day 1

## PROCEDURE

**DAY 1**
Combine all the ingredients for the sourdough and let rise for 12 hours at room temperature.

**DAY 2**
Put all the ingredients for the autolysis in the mixing bowl. Knead for 4 minutes at low speed. Cover the dough with cling film to prevent it from drying out. Perform an autolysis of 20 minutes.
Knead the chocolate, salt and sourdough into the dough at high speed until they are fully incorporated, about 3 minutes.
Let the dough rest for 10 minutes in the mixing bowl.
Stretch and fold your dough three times, each 30 minutes apart.
Let the bread rise for approximately five hours, until it has nearly doubled in volume.
Shape the dough and place it in a floured proofing basket covered with a kitchen towel. Let it rest overnight in the fridge.

**DAY 3**
Place the dough on a baking sheet. Score the bread and then bake it for 15 minutes at 235 °C; reduce heat to 220 °C and bake for a further 30 minutes.
Ensure that there is sufficient steam in the oven during baking.

# ZEBRA BREAD

Zebra sourdough is a bread that not only tastes great, but surprises. By colouring a portion of the dough with squid ink or cocoa powder and rolling it, we create a striking black-and-white pattern reminiscent of zebra stripes. With squid ink, we get a subtle briny note that does not overpower. This bread will really steal the show on a table, and it's ideal with seafood, smoked fish, or as a dazzling aperitif with olive oil and lemon. It takes a little extra effort when shaping, but the result is extremely memorable. A bread that sells itself, both aesthetically and gastronomically.

**DAY 1**

**Ingredients for the preparation of the white stiff sourdough**

15 g sourdough starter
45 g wheat flour
20 g water
7 g sugar

**Ingredients for the preparation of the brown stiff sourdough**

15 g sourdough starter
45 g wheat flour
20 g water
7 g sugar
5 g cocoa powder or squid ink

**DAY 2**

**Ingredients for the mixing bowl**

230 g wheat flour
20 g sugar
110 g milk (45 °C)
50 g egg
5 g salt
20 g butter

**Ingredients to be added to the two separate doughs**

87 g white stiff dough
92 g brown stiff dough

**Ingredients for the cocoa paste**

10 g cocoa powder
15 g water

## PROCEDURE

**DAY 1**

With the dough hook, knead all the ingredients for the two stiff sourdoughs and let rise, in two separate containers, for 8 hours at 27 °C.

**DAY 2**

Combine the ingredients for the cocoa paste and set aside.
Put all the ingredients except the butter in the bowl of a mixer. Knead for 8 minutes at low speed. Add the butter and knead for 6 more minutes at high speed until all the butter is incorporated. Divide the dough into two parts of 218 g each. Knead the risen white stiff sourdough through one part and the risen brown sourdough, along with the cocoa paste, through the other part, until fully incorporated. Let both doughs rest for 15 minutes. Roll the two doughs out into rectangles of 25 x 35 cm and put one on top of the other. Roll up and transfer to a greased baking tin. Cover the dough with cling film to prevent it from drying out. Let the dough rise for approximately 5 hours at 28 °C until it has nearly doubled in volume.
Bake the bread at 180 °C for 40 minutes.
Ensure that there is sufficient steam in the oven during baking.

# OERBLOEMPJE, THE "ANCIENT FLOWER"

This is a festive alternative to a baguette. It's made up of two parts: a firm, circular dough with a hole through the middle, and a second, decorative dough placed on top like a crown. During baking, the lower layer will open up like flower petals and a breathtaking flower motif will emerge, as if the bread itself is coming to life in the oven.

**DAY 1**
**Ingredients for preparing the sourdough**
20 g sourdough starter
40 g rye flour
40 g water

**DAY 2**
**Ingredients for the mixing bowl**
670 g wheat flour
430 g water
13 g salt
3 g baker's yeast
100 g risen sourdough from day 1

**Topping**
olive oil

## PROCEDURE

**DAY 1**
Combine all the ingredients for the sourdough and let rise for 12 hours at room temperature.

**DAY 2**
Place all ingredients in the bowl of a mixer.
Knead for 8 minutes at low speed and 6 minutes at high speed or until the dough temperature reaches 23 °C. Divide the dough into one part of 960 g and one of 250 g. Cover the dough with cling film to prevent it from drying out.
Let each dough rest for 10 minutes. Transfer the 250 g dough to the fridge.
Stretch and fold the 960 g dough. Stretch and fold again after 30 minutes, and then again 30 minutes later.
Let rise at room temperature for approximately one and a half hours; then set this dough in the fridge for 2 hours.
Remove the 960 g dough from the fridge and place it on a floured work surface. Make a hole in the middle and stretch it out a little with your hands to form a larger circle. Place it on a baking sheet and coat the top with olive oil.
Remove the 250 g dough from the fridge and roll it out until it will cover the entire circle of the other dough. Place this dough on top of the 960 g oiled dough.

Sift some flour over the top for an artisan look, and bake at 235 °C for 15 minutes; then lower the heat to 220 °C and bake for a further 30 minutes.
Ensure that there is sufficient steam in the oven during baking.

# ROUGE DE PROVENCE

Rouge de Provence is an ode to the south of France: a robust sourdough bread in which I replace some of the water with red wine. The result is a bread with a vivid colour, pronounced flavor and lightly fruity aroma. Using a full, spicy red wine will give you a bread with a complex, earthy undertone, perfect to combine with cheeses, paté or roasted vegetables. The name is a reference to the fiery south and the beauty of Provencal herbs. This bread is not so much a recipe but an experience. A luxury bread for those who are not afraid to experiment.

**DAY 1**
**Ingredients for preparing the sourdough**
20 g sourdough starter
40 g rye flour
40 g water

**DAY 2**
**Ingredients for the autolysis**
300 g wheat flour
200 g spelt flour
150 g water
200 g red wine

**DAY 2**
**Ingredients to add after the autolysis**
13 g salt
100 g risen sourdough from day 1

## PROCEDURE

**DAY 1**

Combine all the ingredients for the sourdough and let rise for 12 hours at room temperature.

**DAY 2**

Put all the ingredients for the autolysis in the mixing bowl. Knead for 2 minutes at low speed. Cover the dough with cling film to keep it from drying out. Perform an autolysis of 30 minutes. Knead the other ingredients into the dough at high speed for 6 minutes or until the dough temperature reaches 23 °C.
Let the dough rest for 10 minutes in the mixing bowl.
Stretch and fold your dough three times, each 30 minutes apart.
Let the bread rise for approximately five hours, until it has nearly doubled in volume.
Shape the dough and place it in a floured proofing basket covered with a kitchen towel. Let it rest overnight in the fridge.

**DAY 3**

Place the dough on a baking sheet. Score the bread and then bake it for 15 minutes at 235 °C; reduce heat to 220 °C and bake for a further 30 minutes.
Ensure that there is sufficient steam in the oven during baking.

# ACKNOWLEDGEMENTS

A book like this doesn't happen by itself. It is the result of years of passion, work, study, failures, starting over, and most of all: the support and inspiration of people who have left their marks on me.

First and foremost, my gratitude goes out to my family. Without their patience, trust and unconditional support, this book would never have happened. They gave me the freedom to dream, to create and to grow. They were there, standing silently behind every page, every bread and every adventure.

To my father: you did so much more than help me along the way. Together we drove from one end of Europe to the other, from mills to bakeries to wheat fields to brick ovens. The drives together were often as valuable as the destinations themselves. We laughed, talked, discovered and worked shoulder to shoulder. This book carries your spirit of wonder and enterprise within it.

To my mother: thank you for your patience, thinking with me, and testing countless recipes with me. Your taste, honesty and enthusiasm were indispensable, and your warmth was always near me, even between the lines.

To my girlfriend, Barbara, I will be forever grateful for her believe in me and feeding my sourdoughs while I was travelling. Barbara always believed in my vision, and she has always been all the psychological support I could ever have wished for when the bakery got busy.

With tremendous gratitude, I also acknowledge the millers at Heetveld, who shared their knowledge, time and love for the craft with me. Their patient explanations of millstones, flour quality and grain types were of priceless value.

Tijs Boelens brought me closer to the world of heritage grains. His deep respect for the soil, for time, and for seed taught me that a good bread doesn't begin at the bakery, but in the field. He bestowed upon me an understanding of strains and traditions, and a vision of agriculture that I will never let go.

Karl De Smedt of the world-famous sourdough library opened my eyes to the immense richness of sourdough cultures around the world. His dedication to preserving these pieces of living heritage inspired me deeply.

To Stéphane van Les pains de Stéphane: *merci pour ta générosité, ton accueil et ton amour du pain.* To me, your passion for pure, honest breads felt like coming home. Our meeting was short, but its impact was huge.

I must also thank Boudewijn Nijmeijer, who I was introduced to via Michel Ernots at the Pastry Academy. His passion for panettone, and that he sent one every year to Michel Ernots, my teacher, in Las Vegas, says everything you need to know about his professionalism and generosity.

I also want to thank Kädi Helstein, who worked closely with me to test and refine some recipes. It was nice to meet a passionate baker and learn more about Estonian culture.

The Pastry Academy in Las Vegas, and specifically Michel Ernots and Amaury Guichon, merit a monumental thank you. Your programme was nothing short of a milestone. A place where excellence and discipline went hand in hand with creativity and precision. What I learned there, I will carry with me forever.

I must thank Stijn Van Kerckhoven for his attentive reading of the manuscript. His critical eye, particularly for language, and his engagement with my thought processes down to the details, made this a stronger book.

I also have much to thank the agricultural school in Melle for. It was there that the foundation of who I am today was laid. It was a place of growth, literally and metaphorically. The programme there gave me hands that want to work and a mind that strives to understand.

And then, there's Karin De Rooy, my Belgian neighbour in Norway and one of my best friends. You were always there to listen to me and help me, and your door has always been open to me. It is nothing short of a blessing to have someone like you in my corner.

Much gratitude and appreciation must also go to Reinier and Jaqueline Klokke, who live in Malataverne in Provence. My first contact with them was through my parents, when I was about one year old. When I made a return visit to these shepherds on their organic farm, around the age of thirteen, their way of life left a phenomenal impression on me. Since then, Reiner and I have corresponded by letter every two weeks. He is something of a mentor to me, and has already imparted a great deal of the wisdom of life upon me. On his small-scale farm, everything that the land produces is reused. The way a farm is meant to be: organic, with respect for human, animal, and life itself.

Thank you, Jan Heyvaert, for the wonderful evenings where we talked about baking bread and so much more, and where a gueuze was certainly not missing.

Finally, I would like to thank all the silent partners in this effort: the graphic designers, the bakers, the farmers, friends, colleagues and readers who helped me, encouraged me, believed in me.

This book is not just a collection of recipes or stories. It is an ode to time, the rhythm of nature, the strength of simplicity, and the miracle of fermentation. Bread connects people. I hope this book will as well.

**www.lannoo.com**

Register on our web site and we will regularly send you a newsletter with information about new books and interesting, exclusive offers.

**Text** Miro Van Vreckem
**Photography** Thierry Van Vreckem
**English translation** Kyle Wohlmut
**Graphic design** Steven Theunis, Armée de Verre Bookdesign

If you have observations or questions,
please contact our editorial office:
redactielifestyle@lannoo.com



D/2025/45/579 — NUR 440-441
ISBN 978 90 599 6072 5